Moon-Phase
Deer
Hunting

I'm A Moonstruck Hunter

The Man in the Moon is startin' to beam,
Cuz he and the hunter are sharin' a dream.
By much more than luck I'll be getting my buck so soon,
For I've found the secret... of huntin' by the Moon.

This moonshine ain't brewed for drinkin',
My hand is steady, my mind is thinkin'.
I'm a moonstruck hunter, no apology,
And I haven't given in to no lunar lunacy.

The hunter and the Moon are becoming a team,
Read all about it, and you'll see what I mean.
I'm under the sun at a key time of day,
But it's the Moon underfoot that's showin' the way.

—David S. Peterson

OUTDOORSMAN'S EDGE®
GUIDES

MOON-PHASE DEER HUNTING

Jeff Murray

CREATIVE
OUTDOORS™

Dedication

To the memory of my favorite dad, James L. Murray, the greatest average man
the world will never know.

Acknowledgments

There are many wonderful people whose input in this landmark work is greatly valued.
You know who you are, and I am eternally grateful for your contributions. I do wish to
single out my loving wife Corie who has endured my werewold tendencies long enough to
qualify as the patron saint of deer hunters. So, Corie, THANKS!

Trade paperback edition first published in 2004 by

CRE**A**TIVE
O U T D O O R S™

An imprint of Creative Homeowner®, Upper Saddle River, N.J.
Creative Homeowner® is a registered trademark of Federal Marketing Corp.

Front Cover Photo: Don Jones
Back Cover Photos: Jeff Murray
Cover Design: Design Source Creative Services
All other photography by Jeff Murray, except: Bob Zaiglin: 5: M.R. James: 17;
George Barnett: 27, 36, 74: Myles Keller: 30, 60, 75, 77: Rob Nye: 54; Tim Irwin: 57;
Pat Reeve: 92; Dwight Schuh: 101; Larry Weishuhn: 122; Jerry Johnston: 124;
Joe Admire: 125; Keith Kavajecz: 130; Cabela's: 157; Patagonai: 158; Russell Thornberry:
183; Mike langin: 183.

Illustrations© 1995 Kollath Graphic Design

Printed in the United States of America
Current printing (last digit) 10 9 8 7 6 5 4 3 2
Library of Congress card number: 2004103764
ISBN: 1-58011-217-X

CREATIVE HOMEOWNER®
24 Park Way
Upper Saddle River, NJ 07458

Foreword

What deer hunter worth his salt lick hasn't gazed upon the sky, wondering about the Man in the Moon? Now we don't have to wonder so much, thanks to Jeff Murray. When we first discussed his lunar theories, I had a gut feeling he was onto something big. From my editor's desk at *Buckmasters*, I'm privileged to work with the country's leading biologists, researchers and journalists. Jeff is certainly among the best. He has a nose for whitetail news and an uncanny knack for sorting the bull from the cow, if you know what I mean.

You won't find any vanilla here—Jeff is one journalist who writes from the heart. Yet he has no qualms about comparing notes with other authorities to get it straight. Take the segment on hunting deer in their beds. Biologists tell us that deer are crepuscular (low-light) in nature, spending the bulk of daylight hours bedded down chewing their cud. Learning everything we can about these daytime lairs will pay handsome dividends, and Jeff teaches us well.

All told, this book takes a lot of mystery out of hunting deer. Punctuated with wit and wisdom, is mandatory reading for every hunter whose heart pounds and eyes water at the sight of one of God's crowning creations, the majestic whitetail. Enjoy!

- Russell Thornberry

About 10 years ago, Jeff Murray tried selling me on the notion that deer movements are linked to the moon. I mean that literally? At the time I was Executive Editor of Outdoor Life magazine and Jeff was one of our State Editors. He was in the business of pitching new story ideas, and I was in the business of shooting them down...unless they were unusually newsworthy. Needless to say I was skeptical. To be honest, there just aren't many deer stories we in the publishing business haven't heard. To make matters worse, this moon stuff seemed a trite topic. Seems hunters are always arguing about it and never reaching a consensus.

But something weird happened to me that changed my thinking, earned Jeff a coveted story slot in our deer hunting issue and lead eventually to the book you're holding in your hand. I recall the situation vividly. He pitched his story to me on a Friday (never a good idea) just a couple of days before bow season was to begin. "Look, Jeff, here's the deal," I said, more wanting to get him off the phone than hear about moon times. "Calculate next week's best moon times for me and I'll keep a log of deer activity. If I see any sort of correlation between what you say and what actually happens, we can talk about a story." Well, I did, he did and the rest, as they say is history. At 8:33 the next morning, as I stood peering out the Great Room window of my New England hunting camp, a gorgeous eight-point buck walked the field edge right toward the house. I was pumped about the prospects of the bow season to come and reached for my log. A few days later Jeff called and I decided to lay a trap.

"Where was the moon last Saturday?" I asked, expecting my ambush to once and for all settle the issue. When Jeff said the "moon time" was 8:30 am, my jaw dropped. He was off by just three minutes! Even though it could have been a coincidence, I decided to give Jeff a chance to tell his story. Today, as Editor-In-Chief of Whitetail Strategies magazine, I run Jeff's annual lunar predictions for the upcoming season. In fact, some years we run several such stories, because Jeff has come up with an interesting theory on how the moon affects the timing of the rut. Reader feedback continues to be strong, and I see no reason to change our format.

And speaking of change, if you're not "hunting by the moon" I recommend you at least keep an open mind. Meanwhile, take good notes and put the many strategies in this book to good use. Jeff is one of the best in the business in coming up with creative deer hunting strategies, and what you're about to read is some of his best work.

Good luck and may the moon always smile over your deer woods!

- Gerald Bethge

Introduction

Every few years a legitimate breakthrough unfolds on the hunting scene. In the 1970s, for example, scrape-hunting became the rage. First we read about primary scrapes, then secondary scrapes; next mock scrapes and scrape lines. Just when we figured we'd "scraped" the bottom of the barrel, rattling in bucks over scrapes came into vogue. We learned about Texas-style strategies and tickling antlers before the rut, rattling during the second rut, grunting before and after the rut, decoying rutting bucks…

And what a rut. Judging from the media coverage—an outdoor writer friend once confided he'd sold two dozen "rut stories" to a single publisher one spring—the subject was more than adequately covered. Still I wonder. Seeing as the breeding season only lasts a couple of weeks, what do we do the rest of the year? Scheme and dream about next year's rut?

Not me. I'll add the Moon's influence to my hunting strategies. And not just during the rut, either. Though I'm definitely a man on a mission during the short but hectic whitetail breeding season, I can't ignore the fact that I've arrowed most of my bigger bucks early and late in the fall when there was no rutting activity. These periods can be productive because deer travel quite predictably to and from bedding and feeding areas. Of course, the secret of timing these travel patterns is an intimate knowledge of the lunar cycle, to which deer are inextricably linked.

This is not to say the Moon is irrelevant during the rut, when bucks tend to be active throughout the day as demand for estrous does exceeds the supply. At this time, all does continue to feed in startling synchronization with the Moon's predictable but complex daily orbit around the Earth. Again, know when the Moon triggers these does to get up and feed (and know where they prefer to feed at such times), and you can keep track of the dominant breeding bucks that are keeping tabs on those does.

In spite of this, climbing out of the rut-crazed rut won't be easy for many hunters. Breaking with tradition takes courage and determination. However, judging by the escalating number of magazine articles and research papers exploring the "lunar effect" on deer and big game, interest in the Moon is waxing.

Which is why I compiled the insights and strategies in this book. I am fully confident that what you're about to discover will forever change the way you hunt deer—and other big game, for that matter. Instead of hunting without regard to the Moon, you'll find yourself following the lead of M.R. James, publisher and editor of *Bowhunter,* who recently told me, "You can bet I'll be including [your ideas] on the Moon in all my pre-hunt planning preparations."

The Man in the Moon isn't an anti-hunter. He can tell you how best to hunt, if you'll just listen. Those who won't are simply gazing at the Moon through the wrong end of the telescope; they'll never realize how big an impact the Moon has in our daily lives.

—*Jeff Murray*

Contents

Chapter 1

THE MOON IS UNIQUE & INFLUENTIAL

Since the dawning of civilization, the Moon has fired man's imagination and challenged his intellect, spawning the extremes of superstition and analytical thought. The annals of Sumerian priests, who charted the Moon's progress in the sky more than 4,000 years ago from their towering ziggurats, represent both extremes. Cuneiform tablets indicate that Mesopotamian sky gazers kept such accurate lunar calendars that they could predict lunar eclipses... yet they worshipped the Moon by rendering premonitions from its ever-changing faces.

In stark contrast, the Scriptures mention the Moon 61 times, proclaiming a beneficial relationship between it and mankind. For example, Deuteronomy 33:17 speaks of "precious things" brought forth by the Moon; Psalm 104:19 and Jeremiah 31:35 reveal a loving God appointing the Moon for seasons and as a guiding light at nighttime; Psalm 121:6 encourages man not to be afraid of the sun by day nor the Moon by night.

Even today the Moon's mesmerizing countenance has a hold on humanity. For example, people in Moslem countries still measure the year by the Moon's cycles, similar to American Indian culture. And in spite of this present age of hybridization and genetic engineering, savvy gardeners religiously consult planting tables updated annually in the *Old Farmer's Almanac*. At the other end of the spectrum are moviegoers who treat themselves to Hollywood's latest version of Bram Stoker's classic, *Dracula*. Perhaps in between are the millions of discriminating anglers who plan fishing trips around favorable Moon periods.

So, like it or not, we're hopelessly hooked on our most dominant companion in the night sky. Moon madness is no less a part of our culture than baseball, bubble gum and blue jeans. But are we flirting with folklore or fact when we seek the Moon's advice on earthly matters? It depends. In some cases, ignorant superstition overshadows common sense, as evidenced by ancient Romans worshipping their Moon goddess, Diana (interestingly, the goddess of the hunt as well as guardian of wild beasts). But just as often, ageless empirical wisdom can be traced to the complex but predictable lunar cycle. Although the final issue may never be resolved in the minds of incurable skeptics, a startling record of scientific inquiries awaits open-minded truth-seekers. If that includes you, and it obviously does, read on.

Lunacy—From Pearls to Man

We begin our exploration with pearls of lunar wisdom. Oysters are well-known to be wired to the Moon as much as any poet, lover or farmer, but is it because of tides, or unseen forces creating the tides? Dr. Frank Brown decided to find out. The pioneering biologist relocated a study group of oysters from a Connecticut seashore to a laboratory near Chicago. After placing the oysters in trays, enough salt water was added to cover their shells. Light and temperature were held constant. During the first two weeks, each oyster continued to open its shell, feeding according to the tides at its former seashore home site. But by the end of the second week, every oyster had changed its "cycle" to feed as the Moon peaked at its highest point over their new location.

Research from California and Texas proves that the lunar cycle can help predict bollworm outbreaks. Dr. Clyde Sartor, an agri-science consultant, helps clients fend off cotton pest infestations—before they get out of hand—with the findings of colleague Dr. Stan Nemec. His dissertation "Influence of Lunar Phases On Generation and Population Cycles of the Bollworm" explains that New Moon periods are bad news for cotton, tobacco, cabbage and beet growers: egg deposition begins to pick up about three days following a Full Moon, peaking around the New Moon.

As an example, bollworms typically don't threaten San Joaquin Valley cotton fields until late July. But during one research year, Dr. Louis Falcon, an insect pathologist at the Berkeley campus, noticed egg populations escalating shortly after the Full Moon of July 26 and peaking near the New Moons of August 7 and again September 9.

We must include birds in our discussion. Recent investigations at Cornell University show that homing pigeons determine direction by observing the position of the sun and Moon in relation to the birds' internal calendars and clocks. How do the pigeons find their way in cloudy weather? It was discovered using electromagnets that they couldn't navigate unless the sun was out. This sensitivity to magnetic fields probably comes from magnetic iron oxide that has been discovered in the tissues of the heads of the birds. Which shouldn't come as a surprise, given the Moon's influence on ocean tides.

The lesser whitethroated warbler is another example of a bird-brained organism functioning just fine in its environment, thanks to benevolent solar/lunar forces. This migrating songbird summers in Germany and winters near the headwaters of the Nile River, in Africa. Amazingly, its internal navigation system allows the vacationing warbler to find its parents thousands of miles away across unfamiliar land and sea—the parent birds take off for Africa ahead of their young brood, leaving the offspring to fend for themselves on a totally unguided trip!

Human behavior doesn't seem to be exempt from lunar influences. Consider studies conducted by psychologists Arnold Leiber and Carolyn Sherin, who researched 4,000 homicides occurring between 1956 and 1970 in Miami and Cleveland. Leiber wrote, "The results were astounding .... murders become more frequent with the increase in the Moon's gravitational force." Interestingly, homicides peaked during Full Moons and again after a New Moon. Leiber theorized that hormonal activity in the brain is affected by solar and lunar gravitational forces—just as ocean tides are caused by the Moon, people are subject to biological tides that can be set on edge by the Moon. "These tides do not cause

2

strange behavior," Leiber conceded. "They only make it more likely to happen."

Skeptics like astronomer Nicholas Sanduleak and psychologist Alex Pokorny disagreed with Leiber, stating that insufficient data led to generalities that, in turn, lead to self-fulfilling prophecies. A leading contemporary psychologist told me (confidentially) that the "Moon debate is on a par with Friday the 13th." However, police reports—generally more copious during certain lunar phases—seem to contradict this point of view. Toss in the records from hospital emergency rooms and observations from establishments that serve alcoholic beverages, and you have to wonder. As the manager of a popular restaurant in a large Southern city recently remarked, "You can just about tell what the Moon phase is by the activity in the cocktail lounge. A full house is bedlam during a Full Moon."

The latest research on "earth tides" is equally compelling. We've long known that the ebb and flow of ocean tides is caused by the Moon. I got a graphic illustration of the Moon's power when I hunted moose along the Alaska coast near Cordova recently. Each morning I had to time my route according to low tides, and I had to return on time to avoid being stranded by a rising Pacific Ocean. Just as Earth's oceans are like clay in the "hands of the Moon," so is our planet's landscape. Thanks to satellite-assisted photography, we now know that the Earth's crust shifts a foot or more when the Moon's electromagnetic force peaks during key lunar periods. Perhaps this force, rather than the Moon's gravitational influence, is a better explanation for human behavior during Full and New Moons. (We're comprised of 80 percent water, after all, in which iron atoms are abundant).

As for fish, the late John Alden Knight founded a fraternity of loyal "Moon anglers" with his Solunar Tables, which are presently published bi-monthly within the pages of the nation's largest-circulation outdoor publication, *Field & Stream*. Not to be outdone, *Outdoor Life* occasionally prints Maori fishing charts; Bassmasters has recently added Rick Taylor's Astro-Tracker; *Game & Fish* publications showcase Dan Barnett's tables; *North American Hunter* recently signed on with Vektor Game Activity Tables... and so it goes.

Mounting evidence suggests that anglers might want to check into lunar tables if they haven't already done so. My friend Kurt Beckstrom, senior editor with *North American Fisherman*, where my fishing column appears in each issue, discovered that approximately 70 percent of all world-record fish were caught at times "when the Moon was exerting a significant influence." Ralph Manns, a respected investigative writer/angler, was recently commissioned by the *In-Fisherman* group, an esteemed team of research-oriented anglers for which I served as field editor, to find out once and for all if the Moon's influence is fact or fiction. After an exhaustive literature search, Manns concluded that there is indeed a lunar/fish connection, provided environmental factors do not intervene.

So we know the Moon influences the physical Earth and some of its inhabitants. Does this include deer? If so, how does it impact deer hunting? Do you have an open mind? If so, you're about to discover that the "lunar connection" is the latest breakthrough in deer and big-game hunting. Join the many astute hunters who have learned to use the Moon to hunt smarter in spite of what naysayers claim. But the intellectual foundation of unbelievers is eroding like a California mud bank. As you're about to discover, even the academic world is catching up with empirical observation.

A Lunar Deer Cycle?

Research biologists have long studied the "lunar effect." Until recently, however, conclusive evidence on a significant deer/Moon relationship failed to materialize. A major constraint was the lack of deer sightings for a statistically valid study. Before the advent of high-tech computerized radio tracking, the job was cost-prohibitive in terms of both dollars and man-hours. For example, retired University of Georgia professor R. Larry Marchinton was forced to shift his focus from Moon-related study because isolating the Moon's influence was a time-consuming, tedious chore.

Another obstacle, I believe, is that investigators focused on the wrong variable—the phases of the Moon. No wonder Al Hofacker, then-editor of *Deer & Deer Hunting* magazine, drew a blank when he tried correlating the four Moon phases with a 1981 survey in which 7,148 deer were sighted during 13,517 hunter-hours on stand.

But eventually pieces of the lunar puzzle began falling into place. The first major clue involved a study of 25 radio-collared trophy bucks monitored from 1985 through 1987 in South Texas. Headed by Texas Tech University biologist Steve Demarais and whitetail management consultant Bob Zaiglin, the study yielded results that broke new ground in many respects. But you have to dig beneath the surface to mine Moon gold.

The pair's extensive background enabled them to interpret and express their data in hunter-friendly terms, first published in the September 1991 issue of *Buckmasters*. "Radio-tracking the bucks was actually a sidelight of our main duty of deer management on the Harrison holdings [107,000-acre Piloncillo] Ranch," Zaiglin told me. "Still, we managed to cull a lot of data that can help hunters [better understand the] Moon."

Of the many insights gleaned from tracking reclusive, mysterious trophy whitetails, one particularly stands out. It was expressed in Zaiglin's revelation involving big-buck activity at dawn and dusk: "[It] most closely approached the typical [low light] pattern when there was a Quarter to three Quarter Moon." Interestingly, the Moonless and Full Moon phases seemed to "break this pattern down." In other words, something about Quarter-Moon phases increased buck movements during the traditional hunting hours around sunrise and sunset. And that something was notably absent during Full and New Moons, when the researchers recorded few bucks up and about apart from limited midday activity and sporadic middle-of-the-night excursions.

The key variable couldn't be light (or darkness). It wasn't changing atmospheric conditions, either. The only viable alternative remaining was Moon position: Quarter-Moons peak in the sky during low-light periods of sunrise and again at sunset. Coincidentally, bucks use the reduced light as cover and are more comfortable with their surroundings at that "Moon time."

A landmark study all but confirms the Moon position theory. One of the most comprehensive telemetry studies ever conducted (assisted by computerized activity collars and continuous monitoring receivers) was completed under the direction of Dr. James C. Kroll, with the School of Forestry at Stephen F. Austin State University at Nacogdoches, Texas. The respected whitetail researcher recorded thousands of movements from two dozen mature bucks and hundreds of does in Louisiana. His findings substantiated the fact that deer

Note the funny gizmo around this buck's neck; it enabled researchers to put the first pieces of the lunar puzzle together.

are "cued to the position of the Moon." When Dr. Kroll decides to release the full details, they're sure to be illuminating.

When I recently asked Dr. Kroll if the Moon's influence is due to gravitational or electromagnetic forces or some sort of internal clock triggering deer, he replied, "Yes, there's a built-in mechanism, as with many other animals, that allows [deer] to cue on the position of the Moon. We definitely see an increase in deer activity when the Moon is directly overhead and occasionally at other times. We're trying to find out why, and I'm forced to rethink earlier biases. The Moon is a significant factor [in hunting], almost as much as the weather."

Ontario woodsman Bill Lanikenen uses a morning Moon to track trophy whitetails in the "bush." It works on Boone and Crockett bucks!

Dr. Kroll's observation on Moon position may be hot news in whitetail academia, but it's old hat to a number of sage hunters, guides and outfitters I've talked to over the years. Take Bill Lankinen, an Ontario logger who is a very successful big-game hunter. Lankinen times his efforts to coincide with a specific lunar period. "It just won't work that well at other times," he says. "The Moon's the key." Keep in mind that Bill has killed more than 30 bucks and 65 moose with this system.

Another tracking expert, Minnesota's Noble Carlson, uses the Moon to predict how close deer will be to bedding areas during a given outing. Carlson is the best deep-woods hunter I've ever met, having killed more than 100 bucks, all but a handful by tracking.

Larry Weishuhn is a former state biologist in Texas and a popular lecturer and consultant who is unusually successful with whitetails mainly because he hunts with the Moon in mind. In 1994, Weishuhn killed eight bucks that scored between 130 and 170 Boone & Crockett points.

Another believer is Hayward Simmons, who manages the Cedar Knoll Club near Allendale, South Carolina. Simmons has hunted this area since the 1960s and farmed it since 1977. An observant hunter, Simmons noticed deer entering fields at certain periods on some days, but not showing up until after dark on others. He began comparing deer sightings with various Moon charts and, sure enough, a correlation unfolded. "One thing led to another," he said. "I kept notes on when deer were harvested in the community, and plotted Moon schedules on the calendar. Then I came up with a glaring statistic: 70 percent of antlered deer were harvested during a two-week lunar period; 37 percent were taken the week before the Full Moon, 33 percent the week following it. Moreover, two-thirds of the bucks were killed in the afternoons." No wonder Simmons hunts religiously by the Moon.

Minnesota Moon hunter Noble Carlson needs a skidder to haul this monster buck out of the back woods.

Many Western outfitters keep a close watch on the Moon when guiding clients. Stan Graf of Desert Outfitters specializes in Coues deer in Arizona, and he correlates "Moon times" with Moon phases. So does Colorado elk outfitter Bill Jackson. The list of Moon hunters grows each season. What you're about to learn is no longer a guarded secret: Hunting by the Moon, not in spite of it, pays!

As The Moon Turns

A basic understanding of the Moon is necessary to help translate its mysterious pull into practical hunting terms. The Moon actually functions with the Earth as a double planet, rather than a distant satellite; an accurate physical representation of the pair would be a basketball next to a tennis ball (the Earth's diameter is about 8,000 miles, the Moon's 2,160 miles). This size comparison is unique in our solar system—the rest of the planets' moons are proportionally smaller, and therefore exert minimal influence on the mother planets. Factor in the Moon's relatively close proximity—a mere 30 Earth diameters away—and it's no wonder we feel its effects on this planet.

The Moon's elliptical orbit complicates matters.

That the Moon is perplexing and often paradoxical is an understatement. The Moon:

• Actually travels from west to east in its orbit around the Earth, yet appears to travel from east to west in the night sky.

• Goes through phases that require mental gymnastics to keep straight; for example, a New Moon isn't visible, and a Quarter-Moon is actually half-full.

• Completes one rotation on its axis in the same time it takes to orbit the Earth (known as synchronous rotation). This is why it keeps the same "face" toward the Earth at all times.

L U N A T I O N

New Moon is 0 days old

Understanding the faces of the Moon
It takes 29.5 days for the Moon to complete a synodic month (lunation), going from New Moon to New Moon. A numbering system was introduced on January 17, 1923, and it serves as a handy reference for predicting the "age" of a given lunation: A New Moon is 0 days old; Quarter-Moon, 7.4 days old; Full Moon 14.8 days; Last Quarter, 22.1 days; and so on.

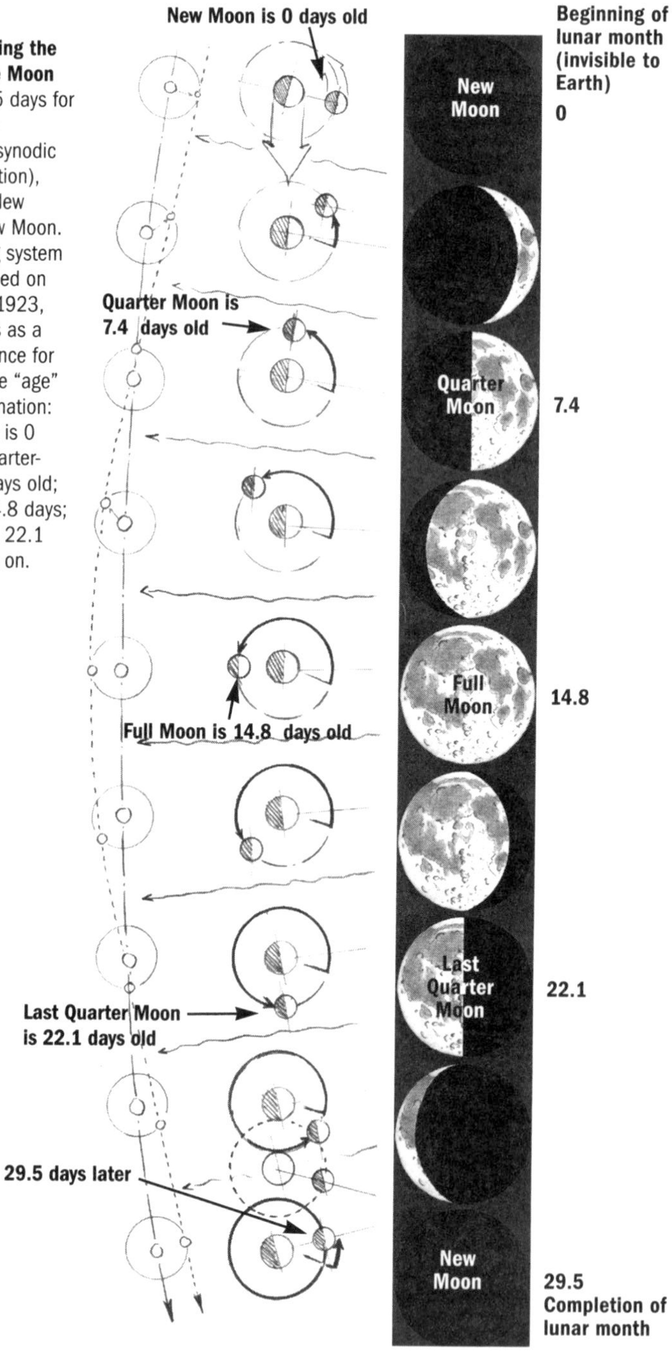

Quarter Moon is 7.4 days old →

Full Moon is 14.8 days old

Last Quarter Moon → **is 22.1 days old**

29.5 days later

	Beginning of lunar month (invisible to Earth)
New Moon	0
Quarter Moon	7.4
Full Moon	14.8
Last Quarter Moon	22.1
New Moon	29.5 Completion of lunar month

- Completes one revolution (around the Earth) in 29 days, 12 hours, 44 minutes and 2.8 seconds, but actually returns to its original position opposite the Earth in 27.3 days.
- Maintains an elliptical (oval-shaped) orbit that varies in distance to the Earth from 225,742 miles to 251,968 miles (238,856 is average).
- Creates tidal friction on the Earth that slows our planet's axial rotation .002 second, thereby lengthening the day that much every century.
- Has a day that differs from a 24-hour Earth day, instead averaging 24 hours, 50 minutes.
- Rises and sets at different times each day—every 24 hours, while the Earth has turned on its axis, the Moon has moved about 12 degrees eastward in its orbit, causing it to rise an average of 51 minutes later each day.

On top of all this, the Moon's height above the horizon varies from season to season. For example, in early spring, the First-Quarter Moon is highest, Last-Quarter is lowest; New and Full Moons are about equal. This changes substantially in the fall: In September, Last-Quarter is highest, First-Quarter is lowest, and a New and Full Moon coincide with the sun's midday high-point. In December, the Full Moon is highest, New Moon is lowest and the two Quarters are in-between. So when we use terms like "directly overhead or underfoot," we really mean "as high [or low] as the Moon gets above [and below] the Earth."

Consider the Full Moon/New Moon controversy in light of the above. Whereas some hunters swear by the New Moon and swear at the Full Moon, others do the opposite. Because we live in an age when doctors don't make house calls, we should keep up with the times and seek the truth about these particular phases.

As you can see, an explicit description of the Moon's motion is quite an astronomical feat. No wonder the Moon's complicated personality has helped keep its secrets under lock for so long. But a well-designed "Moon guide" can easily change that. ○

Chapter 2

ZONED OUT

W hen Native Americans kept track of seasons, many Moons ago, they didn't need computer-generated astrological tables. Time was as endless as game was abundant. Today's hunters, on the other hand, must budget their time as conscientiously as their money. To avoid the painfully familiar "you should have been here last week" syndrome, contemporary hunters need to know the Moon's daily positions in the sky (ideally expressed in hours and minutes, rather than astronomical coordinates). Keeping up with the times is the cornerstone of planning a successful hunt.

MOON TIMES—THE RIGHT TIME

More than any other lunar event, the Moon peaking in its daily orbit foretells deer movement patterns. As Dr. Kroll pointed out in the October 1994 issue of *Outdoor Life*, "Hunting factors are really in your favor when the Moon is straight overhead."

What about Moon phases? Well, it's time to phase them out. Whereas they serve as a general guide for tracing the Moon's ever-changing arc in the sky, hunters really need a handy reference tool to track the Moon accurately. The chief advantage of a "Moon guide" is for trip planning. I and many of my acquaintances have successfully mapped out hunts months, even years, in advance by taking advantage of favorable lunar periods and avoiding more difficult ones.

The first thing to keep in mind is that not all lunar charts are created equal. Some are cumbersome to read (I lost the directions for a particular model and couldn't remember how to interpret the information). Others add spurious

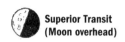

Superior Transit
(Moon overhead)

Your position on the Earth

Inferior Transit
(Moon underfoot)

When the Moon peaks at its superior transit most directly overhead, it exerts its maximum influence upon the Earth's inhabitants; a similar effect occurs about 12 hours and 25 minutes later, when the Moon swings underfoot to its inferior transit. These positions are typically expressed in astronomical coordinates that can be converted into times of the day.

information that may or may not affect fish but doesn't apply to deer and big game. (I'm not interested, for example, in the Moon's right or left-angle position to the Earth, nor am I concerned about after-dark Moon times when I can't hunt.) Still other charts are too general for orchestrating daily game plans for whitetails: Instead of listing exactly when the Moon peaks for the central meridian of a given time zone, a 1 1/2 to three-hour period is typically listed.

Until the advent of the Deer Hunters' Moon Guide™, finding a hunting table with specific Moon times was next to impossible. The Moon Guide™ predicts to the minute when the Moon peaks overheard or underfoot for the middle of the Central Standard Time Zone. This means the times are accurate for the middle of all other time zones as well. (Incidentally, hunters located near time zone boundaries will want to fine-tune the Guide. Check local hunting regulations listing sunrise and sunset times. Or simply add one minute for each 12 miles traveled west and subtract one minute for each 12 miles traveled eastward of your Time Zone's central meridian. For example, if the Moon peaks over your deer stand at 8 a.m., it wouldn't peak over your buddy's stand, located 50 miles to the west, until 8:04.)

Ruminate On This

At this point you may be wondering why ungulates (deer, elk, sheep, moose and so on) feed according to two specific Moon times and not randomly throughout the day. A clue lies with a distinguishing characteristic of this class of animals—their unique stomachs. Grazing prey are designed to feed in haste to reduce exposure to danger, then retreat to the safety of cover to "bed and chew their cud." Understanding the ungulate's digestive system helps explain why two major daily lunar influences come into play.

Deer, once considered browsers of fibrous stems and branches, are also grazing ruminants (like cattle). A four-part (rumen, reticulum, omasum, abomasum) stomach allows them to digest and metabolize foods that other animals cannot. Food—from forbs to fruit, from legumes to tree limbs—is consumed very rapidly (practically swallowed whole) before it is stored in the rumen, the stomach's largest chamber. Eventually the nutriments are regurgitated, remasticated and reswallowed. In fact, microbial breakdown is actually promoted by food moving back and forth from the rumen to the reticulum in this rather strange manner.

Deer can eat so much at one feeding that a full rumen and reticulum may account for as much as 10 percent of the animal's live weight (the rumen alone can easily hold 10 quarts of food). The lining of the rumen consists of papillae, tiny string-like projections one-half-inch long that number about 1,600 to the square inch. The reticulum holds less than a quart and looks like a honeycomb. Hard-core digestion actually begins in the omasum, which has 48 "lobes" of different sizes and shapes that act as strainers. The abomasum is completely the opposite—smooth and slippery. An adult deer also has about 65 feet of intestines, and it takes 24 to 36 hours for food to pass through the animal.

This cud stuff is quite a process. Renowned wildlife photographer Len Rue III has studied cud-chewing extensively (as he has just about every other aspect of whitetail behavior). "I have found that they masticate each piece of cud with about 40 chews," he says. "This takes, on average, 45 seconds. This masticated cud is then reswallowed and a new one is regurgitated. It requires from six to eight seconds for the cud to go down and the next cud to replace it in the mouth. You can see the cud from quite a distance—each is about the size of a lemon."

Interrupting this natural process can spell danger. A satiated deer deprived the opportunity of chewing its cud risks severe sickness or even death. Enterprising Ukrainian deer hunters in Saskatchewan and Manitoba have discovered a clever strategy for capitalizing on this biological fact of life. After locating a good buck feeding in a wheat or oat field, the hunter allows the animal to fill its stomach at least 20 minutes to a half-hour. Then the chase is on. Once on track, the hunter doesn't stop for a moment, not even for a quick cup of coffee. As often as not, by the end of the day he gets his buck. During the chase he hopes to find a clue to the deer's whereabouts—regurgitated digestive matter. When he finds it, he knows the buck is on its last legs, likely bedded in a nearby pocket in hopes its pursuer will pass by unawares. With skill and patience the hunter can literally walk up to the bedded buck.

Studies substantiate this strange phenomenon. Unlike carnivores and omnivores, deer feed rhythmically, chewing their cud during alternating periods of rest. While researching the heart rates of whitetails, Cornell University's Dr. Aaron Moen discovered that deer spend about 70 percent of their time bedded during the day. This can be interpreted that deer hole up more for digestive purposes than for rebuilding from muscle fatigue.

Bob Zaiglin has observed deer on a near-daily basis for more than 20 years, and he sees strong feeding movements every 12 or so hours, with a notable exception. "The only kink to this is artificial feeding in the Hill Country of Texas," he says. "Regardless of the Moon phase

This bedded buck is chewing its cud— in this case, regurgitating, remasticating and reswallowing acorns that fell from nearby oaks. Research indicates that deer spend 70% of their time bedded down.

Deer belch to eliminate gasses such as methane and carbon dioxide—byproducts of microbial fermentation in their abomasum and small intestine.

or Moon position, deer literally leap out of the brush at the sound of the [feeding] truck. Bucks are more reticent, but once they become hooked on the vocalization associated with feeding, they seem to plan their day around it. It's uncanny. This suggests that deer can be conditioned to feed out of synch with their natural link to the Moon."

Suburban deer represent a similar example. Human activity—vehicular traffic, joggers, dog-walkers, sight-seers—predictably peaks during early morning and late-afternoon hours. Deer respond with suppressed activity at these times.

Another factor that can alter a deer's predictable lunar feeding cycle is a strong weather front. As the animals sense the impending loss of feeding opportunities, they chow down. Also, intense hunting pressure can shift feeding periods toward evening hours. Nevertheless, deer feed in remarkable conformity to the Moon's superior and inferior transits about 70 percent of the time. Hundreds of hunters, after comparing deer sightings to respective Moon times, wrote me confessing their conversion from skepticism to fanaticism: Hunting by the Moon may be heresy in their deer camp, but it's not lunacy.

Moon Spots™—The Right Place

The Deer Hunters' Moon Guide™ is more than a Moon table; it's a legally protected system that takes Moon hunting to the next level. Instead of merely listing when deer and other big-game animals are likely to be moving to feed, the Guide indicates where to set up at those times. Savvy Moon-hunters have learned to rotate hunting locations to jibe with ever-changing Moon times. I've coined a little saying that sums up the significance of this breakthrough: Being at the wrong place at the right time isn't much better than being at the wrong place at the wrong time.

Now the key to getting the most out of Moon times is first realizing that deer spend 90 percent of their time in three distinct areas: feeding and bedding areas and "transition belts" connecting the two. In some situations, a general area may meet a buck's feeding and bedding needs. Traditional deer yards in severe weather come to mind; so does the brush country of South Texas and the deep woods of the Upper Midwest and Canada. But, as a general rule, deer typically travel a considerable distance between the feeding and bedding zones, thus setting up a third zone: transition belts.

What about so-called breeding territories? This is an unfortunate misnomer. Rutting areas are usually concentrated near primary bedding areas and therefore don't qualify as a distinctly unique area. A buck doesn't say, "Hey, Debbie Doe, let's mosey over to that scrape line on Estrous Ridge where we

14

can, you know, have some privacy." To the contrary, bucks breed does wherever does happen to be when they're receptive. And don't forget, dominant bucks often lead does away from areas of normal deer traffic to isolate them from rival bucks. The misunderstood concept of "breeding territories" has led to many a failed game plan. No matter how you slice it, there are only three basic zones deer frequent on a predictable basis, and this forms the foundation of hunting by the Moon.

So let's take a closer look at this trio of "Moon spots." The Man in the Moon sees to it that each area has its glory period during a typical lunation, and if we know ahead of time when it will occur, we'll know precisely where to set up as well as the best method to tackle the situation. ○

It's not the right time if it's the wrong place,

And it's not the right place if it's the wrong time.

Time will tell if it's the Time and Spot,

It'll all fall in place… if it's not for nought.

The Deer Hunters' Moon Guide™ lists exact Moon times for the middle of the Central Standard Time Zone. This puts all hunters in North America in the ball park, regardless of their location. The weatherproof seven-inch dial is easy to operate. Spin the outer wheel to a chosen date to find when deer and big game feel the urge to feed; this, in turn, calls up a key hunting location for that Moon time.

A detailed illustration on the flip side of the Moon Guide™ shows how to rotate hunting locations, or Moon Spots™, according to each day's best Moon time(s).

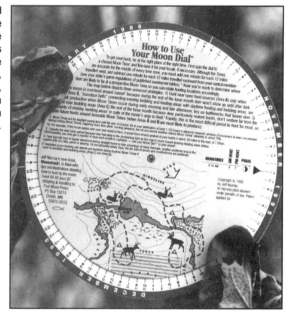

M.R. James, founder and editor of *Bowhunter*, with a dandy Montana buck arrowed in November, 1994. M.R. "had his doubts" but "gradually became a believer" after testing out the Deer Hunters' Moon Guide™ system.

Chapter 3

SCOUTING WITH THE MAN

IN THE MOON

"The lazy man does not roast what he took in hunting,
But diligence is man's precious possession." Proverbs 12:27

A nanosecond is one-billionth of a second—about the time it takes me to recognize the importance of scouting. Don't take my word for it, though. Listen to "Iron Mike" Weaver who, at this writing, has 35 trophy whitetails entered in the Pope and Young record books. That's right, 35 and still counting! Weaver owns his own automobile repair shop and schedules work around deer hunting, especially scouting. Though this Virginia bowhunter knows as much as anyone on how to get within spitting distance of cagey whitetails, he's pretty old-fashioned when it comes to scouting.

"It's tempting to cut corners and spend extra time hunting instead of observing," he says. "But it's a monumental mistake to hunt big bucks pre- maturely. You have to figure them out first or they'll figure you out first."

When you're tempted to give up prematurely or cut that seemingly insignificant corner, remember one of Weaver's hunts that involved two weeks of watching and absolutely no "shooting." The following year, however, he managed to arrow four record-book bucks from the same spot. There's just no such thing as failure when it comes to scouting. Call it something tried that didn't work out the way you planned, but don't label your lack of success failure. As my Dad used to say, "Better to try and fail than not to try at all. In due time you, too, shall reap the rewards."

Pre-hunting

I define scouting simply as patterning deer before they pattern me. Consider it pre-hunting, similar to the methods professional anglers use to "pre-fish" a body of water before a big tournament—as quickly as possible they must assemble clues that unlock the fishery. Likewise, you must find out what makes a particular animal tick. Your biggest obstacle is figuring him out before he's onto you—once a buck gets wind of your presence, the party's pretty much over. In

"With 35 Pope and Young bucks (and still counting) Mike Weaver knows the scouting game as well as anyone."

spite of what some "experts" say, you never want to get into a game of cat 'n' mouse with a mature buck—you're better off hunting traveled routes than so-called escape routes.

To be sure, there's a difference between scouting hard and scouting smart. Prudent paperwork can save miles of legwork.

To get to first base, I suggest a handy "overlay map." As a former land-use planner, I've worked with every conceivable visual aid—from orthographic maps to three-dimensional aerial photos (viewed with a stereoscope). None, however, has enabled me to map out deer country as efficiently as the overlay procedure I'm about to disclose.

To cut to the chase, sandwich together a topographic map and an aerial photograph (make sure they're the same scale). Start with the time-honored topographic map. Its contours connecting areas of equal elevation show "relief" in surprising detail. A piece of flat paper depicting a real-world scene requires you to visualize somewhat, so keep in mind the following:

- The scale of the map is at the bottom. The 7.5-minute quadrangle (1:24,000 scale) is the most handy (an inch equals .38 mile).
- A square mile is known as a "section" and equals 640 acres.
- Black squares are generally occupied buildings; open squares are outbuildings such as barns, garages and sheds; new buildings are usually red or purple.
- Green is vegetative cover (from bushes to trees); white is open (from bogs to cultivated fields).
- The unique blue marsh symbol indicates bogs that could range from open teaberry to thick reeds to willows, tag alders and second-growth brush.
- The contour lines on the above scale indicate a rise or fall of 10 feet.
  Now start looking for these details:
- In relatively flat habitat, zero in on brushy creek beds. (If there's a contour line on each side, the bed is fairly deep and could attract transition-time

movement.)
- Ribbon cover connecting larger tracts of timber is equally enticing to deer, and elbows in the contours (or cover) constrict deer at the joint of the "L."
- In hilly terrain, learn to identify points, fingers, saddles and benches.

Try to find a local commercial source so you can browse at your own clip without shelling out $3 to $4 every time you need to examine an adjacent quadrangle (look up "Printing" or "Maps" in the Yellow Pages). Otherwise you'll have to start with a phone call to the U.S. Geological Survey (1-800-USA-MAPS). Hopefully your nearby map source also stocks aerial photos. If not, visit the closest planning agency or government field office—state natural resources department or Forest Service and Fish and Wildlife Service branch.

By the way, "soil maps" produced by the USDA Soil Conservation Service (SCS) are an excellent resource for trophy deer hunters (other factors remaining equal). If you've ever wondered why a certain drainage system or belt of land seems to produce better racks than another one just a few miles away, it's probably the soils.

For example, biologists know that sandy soils lack nutrients like calcium and phosphorous necessary for optimum antler development. More important, a fertile soil will produce vegetation with a higher percentage of protein—the key ingredient to growing larger racks. Because soil types are listed on the SCS maps, at a glance you get a good indication of the area's nutritional potential. These maps are a lot more helpful than Pope and Young and Boone and Crockett record books, which, at best, give county-by-county statistics. Factor in glaciers and floods, that distribute nutrients in a haphazard manner across North America, and you're looking at a huge time-saver.

A classic example of the significance of soils is the black belt phenomenon in the Southeast. This east/west swath of highly nutritious soils accounts for some dandy bucks in Alabama, where on lands outside of the "antler zone," hunters are lucky to raise bucks with racks much wider than 14 or 16 inches. Naturally, a conscientious program of "doe management" must also be applied in regions like this where deer tend to propagate themselves beyond the carrying capacity of the land.

Trophy hunters should also seek out areas with expanding deer herds, ideally where populations are about one-half the carrying capacity of the land. The notion of innumerable wide-racked bucks in a bumper-to-bumper deer herd is a pipe dream. Also know that antler growth levels off visibly at the $2\frac{1}{2}$ to $3\frac{1}{2}$-year mark if the buck-to-doe ratio isn't balanced (and there isn't more than enough nutrition to go around). So look for areas with low hunter pressure where bucks can reach the golden antler-producing age of four or more years.

Now for a slick trick. Have the topo and aerial photo enlarged at a quality print shop so that a particular area covers one square mile on an $8\frac{1}{2}$ x 11-inch piece of paper (again, maintaining the same scale). Now you can overlap the two against a bright light (light table, living room window, windshield of your car) and read vegetative cover and elevation at a single glance. Of course, you can always switch back and forth if you want to analyze a particular detail, but with them together, you get quite a story on one versatile working map.

Which leads to another point. You can locate likely daytime bedding areas by finding dark spots on the aerial photo and slopes on the contour map. If these spots are within with a mile or two of prime food sources, you're almost home free.

The significance of daytime bedding areas cannot be understated. They're the hub of a buck's daily routine. Every evening he leaves; every morning he returns. What a clue! Incidentally, be sure to identify primary areas for prevailing winds as well as secondary sites for variable winds. And don't forget about hunting pressure. Invariably, out-of-the-way pockets become more productive than easy-access bedding areas as the season wears on.

The next step is to locate topographical barriers that might constrict or encourage deer to travel along key routes, or corridors. During the day, deer avoid certain danger zones—particularly open areas void of cover—but they also avoid tight spots that make travel difficult. As you piece together travel patterns, don't overlook the fact that human traffic tends to steer deer around certain areas, too.

Tom Indrebo studies a saddle, located in Wisconsin's Buffalo County, on his homemade map. By enlarging section 36, subtle details leap off the page.

Like the seams of a football team's zone coverage, bucks like to run "pass routes" around and between the "cornerbacks of human activity." So consider roads and trails when mapping out deer country. Let's face it. Hunters are basically lazy. No more than one out of 100 two-legged predators ventures farther than a half-mile from the nearest two-track.

As you study the areas deer skirt—such as fields, clearings, beaver ponds, rivers, lakes, swamps and bluffs—and those they dive into—such as roadless areas and difficult access points—several "buck corridors" will eventually emerge. Now all you need to know is whether a good buck or two made it through the hunting season in one of the areas you've selected. Then you can hunt with confidence...

Old Antlers Shed New Light

The woods smelled different—kind of sweet, kind of musty—when a sudden breeze swelled out of the southwest. I just had to stop and drink it in, as did my daughter, Janell, who often accompanies me on my early spring vigils. Yep, we were hunting for shed antlers and soaking up every moment.

"Found one, Dad," Janell shouted gleefully.

"One what?" I teased.

"A rack," she said, somewhat annoyed at me playing dumb. She knew she was as good as I was at this game, probably better. What did I think she'd found, a dead skunk?

"That ain't no rack, it's an antler," I said, seizing the opportunity to spoon-feed some whitetail lore to my favorite young lady. "Find the other half, and we'll have an honest-to-goodness rack." With that, Janell scurried for a heap of compacted, dried leaves and kicked at it. Then she scooted over to another pile and kicked again. And so went our day. We built a few memories while I managed to piece together another missing part of the whitetail puzzle. I knew that if I could find the drops of a good buck, more than likely he'd be fair game the next fall.

An added bonus of this pastime is that it fills a vacant niche in my calendar—after late-season bowhunting and before spring turkey and bear seasons. It can do the same for you.

As with many endeavors, timing is everything. Although it's impossible to predict when bucks will drop their headgear, a few generalities hold true. For

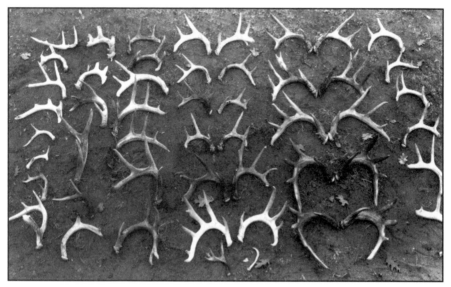

Antlers cast a bewitching spell on many hunters, including me! The sheds from an old buck hanging out in the same general area really boost my confidence.

one, the farther north you go, the sooner racks seem to hit the ground. For another, the better the local food supply, the longer bucks tend to hang onto their racks. (The "disposable" head adornment of the Cervidae family is unique among the animal kingdom in that the rack only grows during the vegetative season. Consequently, droughts can severely hamper antler development.)

But there are so many local variations that you must remain flexible and keep current with conditions. A case in point involves a deer yard I visited several years ago. I photographed the thicket where the whitetails had instinctively gathered in hopes of documenting the harsh elements' toll on the herd. I was amazed at the diversity among the bucks: Some were in full-rack splendor; others sported only one side of their rack; still others were as bald as eagles. My notes reflect that the last rack was shed a full eight weeks after the first one; a particularly impressive 12-pointer hung onto his headgear until late March.

The casual whitetail student interprets this as meaning that the best time to get in the woods for sheds is when it's convenient. Fanatics see it differently:

If competition in a given area is keen, better get out often, possibly revisiting potential hotspots if you want to score on a matched set. Some guys get so "antlerized" that they hit the woods in waves, organizing a telephone network. Indeed, a buddy system can save wear and tear on the nerves and keep your vehicle's mileage down.

Snow depth can be a factor. In the upper Midwest, where I do most of my shed hunting, a crust of refrozen snow camouflages antler tines well. And busting through knee to thigh-high drifts makes shed hunting more like work than play. Ideally, try to time shed-hunting forays for when the snow is almost, but not quite, gone. Then a bleached, bone-white tine protruding out of the earth is

I photographed this buck in a deer yard shortly after he dropped half of his rack. I returned a month later and collected the other half.

easy to spot—even for a teenaged girl. Don't wait too much longer or rodents, especially squirrels, will be out in full force, gnawing away at the calcium-rich drops.

Interestingly, research shows that deer south of the snow belt begin antler development about the same time as their northern counterparts—mid-March to April. As a result, antler shedding is surprisingly uniform across the whitetail's range, largely due to increasing daylight and prolactin secretions. However, if you live a considerable distance from the area you intend to scout, a quick phone call to a natural resources field office can help fine-tune your timing.

The where-to aspect of shed hunting is an inexact science. As a friend remarked, shed hunting is like picking mushrooms. "They're where you find 'em," he said. "No rhyme or reason to their whereabouts." I'd say he's at least half-correct. An open field could cough up state-record sheds as easily as a river bottom. And a thicket in a residential area is just as likely to produce as a cattail slough bordering a farm several miles away. Still, there are good spots and there are better spots.

If you are just into sheds and not necessarily using them to target a huntable buck, some of the best spots in the country right now are in suburbia. Deer are creatures of the fringe. Housing developments spreading outward like spokes of a wheel don't curb nearby deer populations that much. To the contrary, when you factor in local laws that typically prohibit the discharge of firearms, deer numbers escalate.

The game of suburban shed hunting is relatively straightforward. Many residents love to watch deer, so they set up feeders to encourage whitetail visitation. In the process, predictable patterns emerge. All you have to do is locate several such feeders and backtrack from them to a thicket or two that deer use to avoid daytime human activity. It could be a cattail slough, grassy drainage ditch or tangled woodlot. The best time to locate these areas is in early winter, when deer trails are most pronounced.

Keep in mind that these areas are under private ownership, so you need to know boundary lines and get permission for access. A plat book or a trip to the city (or township) assessor's office will help identify landowners. Or you could just knock on a few doors. Which reminds me: The sport of shed-hunting provides an excellent opportunity to convey the hunting heritage message to non-hunters who outnumber hunters in the 'burbs 10:1. You never know where these contacts might lead...

In the big woods during years of below-average snowfalls (actually the rule rather than the exception the last decade or so), look for sheds in lowland areas and not necessarily in traditional yarding areas. Certainly don't rule out feeding areas, either. Thick cover is readily available in the big woods, and deer often bed within yards, not miles, of food sources such as fields, cut-overs and slashings associated with active logging operations.

In agricultural areas and semi-arid regions, river bottoms get the nod because vegetation is concentrated mainly along creeks and drainages. So-called ribbon cover is the easiest whitetail habitat to shed-hunt in. Again, you know where deer are likely to spend most of their time in such spots so you can pretty much rule out low-percentage areas.

Transition habitat, with its characteristic mixture of croplands and wood-lots, can be tricky. Not only do deer spend a considerable amount of time in Conservation Reserve Program (CRP) plots, but they traverse open fields after sundown. If it's "that time," they could drop an antler or two just about anywhere along the way. You might want to glass plowed fields before heading into the thick stuff.

Sheds are valuable (perhaps too valuable in this age of commercialism). Who doesn't relish the thought of running their fingers along the thick main beams, counting the burrs of the brow tines, inspecting the pedicels? Like fingerprints and snowflakes, the Creator made each antler truly unique. So what are you going to do when you accumulate a mess of "dust-collectors," as my wife calls them? Don't store them away in the rafters of your garage. Instead, consider a mount like the one my friend Mike Kohler had made up for his young son, Ross. The youngster's crowning pickup, a matched pair grossing about 160 Boone and Crockett points, graces the family's fireplace mantle. The attractive plaque gives the date Ross found the set, and each side can be removed—for toying with, of course—by unlatching a metal clasp. I agree with Kohler that sheds ought to be preserved the way they were found—no putty, no burnt umber and certainly not mounted on another deer's cape.

If you've discovered the spoils of decoying deer, save a not-so-matched set for a buck decoy. Try several pairs, experimenting to find which ones attract/spook deer in your area (here's betting you won't want to go too small or too big).

Sheds serve another useful purpose: for rattling up bucks during the hunting season. Again, you'll have to experiment because some sheds crack loudly whereas others "tinkle" with a muffled, hollow ring.

Just because sheds have been cast by their maker doesn't mean their useful life is over. For some lucky relics, it's just the beginning.

The Bachelor Party

The month of August reminds me of a singles' bar—it has the appearance, but rarely the results, of a rewarding relationship. Indeed, when bucks group together in so-called bachelor groups, they tease hunters by feeding in broad daylight in open alfalfa fields (up north) and bean and milo fields (further south). Although this is an excellent time to observe big bucks from a distance—perhaps confirming what shed antler scouting has revealed—it isn't a reliable indicator of where those deer will be come hunting season.

"The bucks will disperse with a few ending up in some fairly distant places," Dr. Kroll says. "The dominant individuals habitually stake out preferred core areas, sometimes a considerable distance from summer loafing and feeding areas."

Late summer and early fall bucks gang together in bachelor groups; however, where you find them now won't be where they'll be during the heat of the hunting season.

Translation? By all means get out the spotting scope and put your number on the widest, heaviest-racked buck in the area. But don't count on him showing up in the same field with his buddies… unless you find his bedroom rubs nearby.

Don't Forget The Moon

As you snoop for whitetail clues, keep track of Moon times when you're afield, especially as the hunting season approaches. This tip alone could save the season. For example, suppose you're driving a backcountry road and notice a set of tracks along the shoulder. Are they heading from open fields toward a patch of woods… or the opposite way? Recall that the lunar cycle (complete phase) repeats itself every 29.5 days. If you find deer traveling along a particular route during, say, a midmorning Moon time, chances are the deer will show up along that same route when the Moon waxes into its next lunation.

Stop and think about this! Should you fail to connect this week, you might have a chance to redeem yourself. Get in the habit of tracking deer activity in accordance with the lunar calendar.

Signs Of The Tines

With general bedding, feeding and connecting corridors identified on your map, it's time to step into the woods. Over the years a ritual of scouting during late winter has evolved for me. Trampled trails and leftover sign are oh-so-obvious and, with the deer season behind me and next year's hunt months away, I won't have to worry about bumping deer out of their daily routine. If you've got

Bucks keep an eye on the Moon, and so should you.

the time and inclination, take advantage of this unique window of opportunity.

What to look for? In a word: rubs. And old ones are just as telling as new ones because a buck will retrace his general comings and goings in successive years. In fact, the best tip-off is a rub line a buck has worked several years in a row. Find a series of trees with two or more rub scars—distinctive oval-shaped "scabs" formed on the bark—and you're probably looking at the handiwork of an older buck (at least three, maybe 4 1/2 years old or more). No wonder my mind does cartwheels when I discover a tree or three with multiple scabs! These rubs are easy to distinguish. For some strange reason, bucks tend to rework a tree or bush from a slightly different angle each year. Rather than polishing the exact same spot, the buck attacks the tree just above the scar, just below it, or off to the side. And this fall the buck could return, if you don't rub him the wrong way.

Rub-scouting in late summer demands a change of plans. Now you should be concerned with an entirely different kind of rub (and it's not the impressive leg-size rubs many hunters go ga-ga over). You want to be rubbed in the direction of reality, not imagination, so let's first rehearse some basic facts about rubs.

Not all rubs are of equal significance to hunters. Whether or not rubs carved out by dominant breeding bucks are territorial markers (reportedly establishing home ranges to "warn" juvenile bucks and potential rivals) is largely academic. From a practical standpoint, rubs can help us locate the bedding areas of mature animals and give insights into possible weak links to their seemingly invincible armor.

The small-rub/small-buck, big-rub/big-buck axiom holds some water, but has been oversimplified. Researchers Larry Marchinton and Karl Miller, after examining 529 rubs in five study areas, found no substantial difference in rub sizes in areas with varying deer age structures; rubs in yearling-dominated habitats were about the same size as those where two out of three bucks were older than a year and a half. Other research suggests that although a big buck may make seemingly small rubs, young bucks are rarely responsible for those impressive scars showing up on eight to 12-inch trees. Also, bigger bucks make more rubs "because they have more to advertise," says retired Michigan biologist John Ozoga.

Whatever you do, don't discount all small rubs. In fact, some of them can tell you more than the imposing, so-called signpost markers I used to drool over. In September, about the only rubs you will find are those made by mature bucks. This really simplifies the rub interpretation game, doesn't it? Again, you have to

I caught this buck in the act of rubbing a mountain maple during the first week of September. Notice that early fall rubs do not resemble larger signpost markers associated with the rut.

know what to look for. "[A buck's first rubs] look more like thrashings than the deliberate [scraping] of tree bark associated with rubs later in the fall signaling the onset of the rutting season," Marchinton says. "If you find a lot of early-season rubs, there's a good chance the age structure of the deer herd could be an older one."

This is why I shift into overdrive as I cruise new territory for early season rubs. Not only is their relative abundance a good reflection of an area's big-buck potential, but it indicates where bucks are probably bedding, because a majority of early rubs are made near the inner sanctum of the bucks' daytime lairs. Studious bowhunters should scout hard in late summer and early fall, before the archery season opens, if they want to intercept the rub-maker when the time is right. (Keep in mind that deer haven't been hunted for several months and are more apt to tolerate minor disturbances before leaves fall and small-game and bird hunters invade the woods.)

This buck is attacking a tree that he worked over the previous fall. A series of trees with multiple-year rubs is an invaluable clue.

Punctuate your field map with every fresh rub you find in September. Again, the ultimate goal is zeroing in on a buck's preferred daytime bedding area. Better get ready for some serious grunt work, though. You won't find these rubs along field edges or in open country like the late-season signpost markers. Instead, head for the thickest foliage you can find. (Remember those dark patches on the aerial photos?) And come prepared for a lot of crawling on all fours—the best way to see under the canopy of leaves and through lush undergrowth. Search for these rubs with the diligence of a pirate digging for buried treasure.

Incidentally, if you strike out, you get a second chance to locate a boss buck with another distinctive type of rub. As the breeding season draws near, signpost rubs proliferate. The latest theory on these large, unmistakable markers is that they are a part of a complex communication system within the sexes as well as between them. When a buck rubs his antlers and forehead on a tree (and licks it repeatedly), he deposits "priming pheromones" that likely serve as a biostimulant to induce ovulation in does. This is one of Nature's remarkable processes. Studies involving pen-raised deer in Michigan and wild deer on the Mt. Holly Plantation in South Carolina show that the absence or presence of these rubs can impact the timing of the rut. Of course, photoperiodism (the diminishing ratio of daylight to dark) triggers hormonal releases in does and determines the general breeding season. But in habitats where breeding bucks are abundant, local does may go into heat as much as two weeks early. (The reverse is also true; a lack of bucks can delay does entering estrus.)

Myles-A-Head

Meet Myles Keller. This easygoing Minnesota bowhunter has more than two dozen Pope and Young whitetails in the record books—more than any other bowhunter. I make this distinction, in spite of the "trophy mentality" that seems to have spread through hunting camps across the country like an electrical storm. (All big game harvested under fair chase principles are prized, especially those taken with a bow.) But because so many "professionals" have emerged of late—often advocating conflicting advice—I feel the public needs some sort of barometer to measure a spokesperson's credibility.

Take fishing. Outdoor writers used to be the primary source of angling knowledge because they had the platform of books and magazines to advance their theories. That information hierarchy changed dramatically when sanctioned fishing tournaments spawned a new generation of credible tournament pros. Though there aren't any "tournament hunters," we do have record books. Those maintained by the Pope and Young Club can be particularly helpful for recognizing prominent members of the hunting fraternity. (Assuming that game-law violators such as Don Lewis and, more recently, Noel Feather don't confuse the issue.)

I'm not the Wizard of Oz empowered to bestow titles, but after interviewing thousands of dedicated hunters and professional biologists, guides and outfitters, I have reached a simple conclusion: Only Myles Keller is a whitetail expert. A

Myles Keller with the smallest of four record-book bucks he arrowed in 1993.

few come close; more than a few are impostors; and most are wannabes. When I penned the first magazine article on Myles back in 1985 (appearing in *Outdoor*

Life, entitled "World's Greatest Bowhunter?"), I suspected he might be in a class by himself. Now I know he is.

To say Myles is miles ahead of contemporary bowhunters is to say Einstein was good at math. So when Myles speaks, I try my best to comprehend the meaning of his message. It isn't always easy. Myles' thoughts on whitetails aren't always mainstream, and he doesn't always tell his audience what they want to hear. "A lot of times a guy will ask me a series of probing questions," he once told me. "I can see him shaking his head as he walks away, thinking, 'That guy doesn't know any more than me.' Too bad he's looking for a secret formula instead of examining his hunting system for weak links."

For the record, Myles makes his living field-testing and promoting bowhunting-related products; contracts with Indian Archery (Xi bows), Scent Shield and Advantage camouflage (a division of Realtree) keep him hopping.

Scout-hunting

Once the season opens, you should continue to scout while you hunt instead of depending on previously scouted deer sign. Scout-hunting is the only zero-impact tactic acceptable for effective trophy hunting. No one has translated this principle into a practical hunting strategy better than Myles.

"It's critical that a buck thinks his Back 40 sanctuary is safe," Myles says. "This means staying out unless I know exactly when and where I can kill him back in there." In other words, the typical strategy of snooping around for rubs and hot scrapes, then hanging a stand downwind and hoping for something good to happen is usually futile for mature animals.

Sounds like a Catch-22: To find rut sign signaling the breeding season you've got to prowl the backwoods, but in so doing you risk bumping the buck out of his bedding area. Well, it is. My association with Myles over the years has caused me to re-evaluate my entire system of hunting whitetails. In the old days, I wouldn't have thought twice about keeping a low profile and playing the wind, figuring if I jumped a buck he wouldn't wind me and should continue his routine. Not any more.

"Bowhunters expecting a legiti-mate shot at an impressive Pope and Young buck have to realize what they're up against," Myles says. "This animal's different from an

Claude Pollington keeps tabs on the rut—without tipping bucks off—by checking the status of boundary scrapes.

alpha doe or a 2 1/2-year-old buck. There are no shortcuts… only extra miles."

This always brings us back to no-impact pre-season scouting: The only way to deal with major-league rut sign is before the hunting season. In short, when nimrods set up on top of rubs or so-called scrape lines, one of two scenarios typically unfolds. The first is failing to map out a buck's core area, resulting in the hunter locating where the animal sojourns infrequently. The second is digging deeper to get a better picture… and spooking the buck.

"Hunting big-time rutting sign is very tempting but most often self-defeating," Myles says. "You're much better off hunting where you can catch the buck entering or leaving." There's no better place to start than a food source, especially when the Moon signals deer to chow down before the sun sets. Of course, scout-hunting will pay off when Moon times force hunters to lay back from food sources. I'm just glad we've got the Moon to show the way. ◯

This buck is heading for the next food source, and so should you: turn the page.

Chapter 4

TIMING FOOD SOURCES

The Moon's overhead in the twilight sky,
The deer are hungry, and so am I.
From my portable Lok-On I can see for a mile,
Here come the deer, single file.

Acorns under red and white oaks,
Greenbrier and aspen shoots there to coax.
Fields of corn, alfalfa and rye,
An unwitting buck wanders by.

I'll take my deer just before dusk,
Won't have to rattle or put out the musk.
"Know when deer are feeding?" asks the Man in the Moon,
"I'll tell you right when: Late in the afternoon."

W   ith long faces resembling Emmet Kelly, the famous circus clown, a trio of hunters slumped in the dark at their muddy Suburban. Where had all the deer gone?

Brothers Tom, Bruce and William had sounded so convincing a week earlier. "We've got four bucks and a dozen does pegged at the corner of two oat fields," Tom had said confidently over the phone. "It's going to be a short hunt. I'll call you to give you the score."

I didn't get a call the next week or the week after, so I phoned Tom and ended up talking to Bruce. I could tell by the tone of his voice that the hunt hadn't progressed as the brothers had planned. "The deer didn't show up until after dark," Bruce said, his voice trailing off. Though I certainly sympathized with him, he had set himself up with the premature boasting. Talk is cheap. Even so, these guys manage to score just often enough to keep up the tall predictions, and the cycle repeats itself year after year.

Which goes to show that field-edge hunting can pay off some of the time. After all, you won't bump any deer on the way to your stand, and it's child's play scouting fields to find where deer are ending up at the end of the day. If only field deer were more predictable...

Well, the Moon's the secret, and it's so simple it's spooky. Here's what you need to know to make the most of this golden opportunity.

Field Of Dreams—Bucks On The Edge

In most habitats, hunters get a green light to hunt near field edges a handful of days each month. The rest of the lunar period they're wasting their time because deer simply won't show up till after dark. If you've ever glassed whitetails munching in broad daylight and returned a week or so later to see them in under headlights, you can blame the Moon. (Recall that it rises, on average, 51 minutes later each day, triggering deer to react about an hour later each day.)

So the first order of business is lining up hunts with Moon times that give deer (or other ungulates) enough time to make it to open food sources before dark. By late-fall, I'm already circling dates that line up with late-afternoon Moon times for the following year's hunts. It takes planning to keep on top of things. For example, October 28 and 29 look good for 1995, but in 1996 a late-afternoon Moon will peak around October 18. It changes like this every year, completing a full cycle about every 19 years.

Manipulate your schedule to hunt this segment of the lunation, no matter what! When the Moon draws deer and big game out of the thickets to feed as

Manipulate your schedule to hunt this segment of the lunation, no matter what—it's as good as it gets!

light diminishes with a setting sun, you'll see more game than at any other period; a Moon time about a half-hour before the sun sets to a half-hour after is as good as it gets.

This should come as no surprise when you figure in the stealth factor. Guide Haywood Simmons likes to hunt fields in the afternoon simply because his hunters spook fewer deer. "We have an extremely long season in South Carolina, running from mid-August to January," he said. "And there's no limit on bucks. Our deer are hunted heavily over five months, and we can't afford to pressure them. That's a tough task for a commercial hunting operation involving many hunters, but hunting fields properly really helps."

Remember that Simmons discovered two-thirds of the hunters in his area were successful in the afternoon? One reason is that morning hunters must navigate in the dark and are more likely to bump deer than their afternoon counterparts. Another reason morning hunters spook a disproportionate number of deer has to do with thermals.

Morning hunters frequently stumble upon deer that are traveling through transition areas as they relocate from evening bedding areas to daytime bedding areas. Like Simmons says, hunting in the afternoon is so much easier because hunters know where deer are at that time: bedded in thick cover. On the other hand, when hunters hit the woods at daybreak, deer could be anywhere—from the edge of open croplands and fencerows, to creek bottoms or halfway up a ridge. Couple our stumbling and bumbling in low light with our impatience to get into position (especially if we've overslept), and it's a wonder we score at all in the morning.

Another key Simmons picked up for hunting field deer comes from an old telemetry study conducted in an adjoining state. It seems deer in the Southeast regularly bed at one end of their home range and feed on the other, especially in habitats that are elongated (two or more miles long and a quarter to a half-mile wide).

Simmons believes that if a deer beds a considerable distance from a food plot during, say, a midafternoon Moon time, the animal is likely to browse confidently in thick cover, perhaps making the field edge by sunset. "The farther deer bed from open fields and food plots, the earlier [the Moon time] you can hunt afternoons successfully," Simmons says. "That's why the week following a Full Moon is usually our most productive time." Makes sense to me. A Full Moon typically peaks underfoot around 1 p.m.—each day peaking a little later—and within a week it's underfoot near sunset hours.

Some tidbits to chew on when considering food sources:

• Hunter pressure can disrupt a cyclical feeding pattern. The more remote a field is, the more deer are likely to visit it before dark. Fields along roads or easy-access routes are usually a different story—any suspicious activity often causes bucks to linger near their beds, feeding on forbs and browse before heading out.

• The nature and extent of connecting cover leading to the field is vital. If cover is fairly sparse, mature bucks typically hole up along the transition zone— draws, drainage ditches, creek bottoms, treelines—and let does and sub-adult bucks serve as sentries. If the other deer make it to the field without spooking, the big boys will ultimately follow. But rarely before.

- Thousands of food items are on the deer menu, and whitetails tend to choose a food source based on its convenience, nutritional value and taste.

  Let's take a closer look at research showing why deer switch constantly from one food source to another:
- Food preference is directly related to the growth stage of a forage, according to Mssrs. Waer, Stribling and Causey, at the Auburn Deer Research Facility. Rapidly growing plants that were at their highest in crude protein and lowest in fiber were selected in controlled feeding experiments.
- During the cool season, small grains—such as ryegrass, oats, wheat and barley—were preferred.
- Crimson clover was chosen when it was most lush, followed by ladino clovers when their peak growth occurred.
- Deer spent about the same amount of time feeding on carefully planted forages (including those mentioned above) as they did on volunteer "weeds" such as blackberry, evening primrose and bahiagrass.
- In another study conducted in north-central Texas, plains prickly pear (cactus) accounted for more than 50 percent of the yearly diet of deer. Meanwhile, browse in the South Texas Plain region constituted the bulk of deer diets, with forbs (during adequate years of rainfall) also ranking quite high.

The bottom line? Know your deer foods and anticipate changes in diet before they occur. Especially be on the lookout for droughts, which tend to follow the 11-year sunspot cycle (the last major drought in the US was 1987-88).

Setting The Stage

Even with a right Moon, perfect wind and ideal weather, a buck worth his rack might not step into the open until after dark. You could be hunting at the right time but at the wrong place, if you insist on perching at the corner of a field. Sometimes bucks scent-check surrounding cover before feeding, forcing slight adjustments in hunting tactics. A case in point is Don McGarvey's new No. 2 Pope and Young Alberta monster (199 5/8 typical points), possibly the biggest bow-killed whitetail in 30 years.

The Edmonton lawyer had set up along a treeline connecting a barley field and an alfalfa field on September 20, 1991. The Moon time was about 8 p.m., and sunset was 7:39 p.m.(legal hunting hours extend 30 minutes past sunset in the province). Heeding the Moon's signal to feed, the buck abandoned its bed in the woods, where aspens were just starting to turn lemony yellow.

McGarvey had guessed right: The buck followed the row of trees, passing within 10 yards of the bowhunter's carefully chosen treestand. A secluded "staging area" during the right Moon time is a deadly combination! Learn to discern these buck-only hotspots by the size and shape of tracks and unusually large droppings (the size of swollen Boston beans). A mixture of cover and small openings makes a perfect staging area, because a buck can nibble on the lush vegetation springing up in the openings, yet feel safe being a jump away from cover.

If a preferred food source is surrounded mainly by a barren landscape, you must backtrack bucks along connecting cover and possibly relocate close to their bedding areas. Even when Moon times coincide with sunset? Yes! And while you're at it, don't overlook CRP plots. Once you pinpoint a hot staging area, don't burn it out—like rub and scrape lines, big bucks rely on these areas year after year. Do the bulk of your scouting in the off-season, backtracking trails from feeding to loafing and staging areas.

Some final thoughts on this thought-provoking subject:

Staging areas are unique: Look for a blend of cover and forbs close to open food sources.

- Always start from a distant vantage point, laying back and erring on the conservative side before edging closer for the kill. The advantage is twofold: scouting while hunting, and increasing odds near converging trails (as opposed to unraveling the maze of crisscrossing trails heading from cover).

- Play the wind—even if it takes the proverbial extra mile—when entering and exiting stand locations. And carry a backpack to avoid overdressing and sweating up or underdressing and getting the shakes. My current favorite is Fieldline's Ultimate Series, of which I helped design (www.fieldline.com; 800-438-3353). This unique pack has storage compartments specifically designed for specific accessories--electronic rangefinder, binoculars, game calls, etc.

- Sudden wind-shifts can destroy a well-orchestrated field hunt, but sometimes you can keep one step ahead of the game. In the Midwest and Canada, for example, unseasonably warm breezes typically reverse themselves once the sun sets. Either wait till the orange ball torches the treetops before entering your stand, or relocate to an alternate stand—previously set up for such occasions—as the cool down-draft reverses.

- Wise old bucks get that way by using their keen noses more than other deer. A favorite trick of heavy-beamed bucks near open food sources is scent-checking the perimeter of fields before setting foot in them. Set up along less-defined "perimeter trails," but make sure you're on an evening and not a morning trail. (Bucks also scent-check heavy cover before they bed down for the day.)

Learn to recognize topography and vegetative cover that forces an approaching buck to compromise the wind slightly (more later).

- Deer get used to familiar farm machinery and trucks, yet spook at the sight of similar-but-different vehicles. If possible, have a landowner or caretaker drop you off with his tractor or pickup.

- Avoid bumping deer near fields after dark at all costs. These deer are spooky enough! Glass the immediate area before leaving. Low-light optics are a must. In addition, you might want to take advantage of Desert Storm "night vision" technology, now available to consumers.

- Avoid predictable behavior that causes deer to "wait you out." Rotate the fields you're setting up near, as long as it doesn't take you out of the immediate area. (I don't recommend hopscotching from spot to spot unless you've got the deer wired.)

Heed all of these pointers, or you'll find yourself playing the ol' cat-and-mouse game that I've already told you is a no-win engagement.

A Nutty Connection

If cropfields and food plots seem to attract fewer and fewer deer, the reason might not be a midday (and midnight) Moon, but rather a distant oak stand. (Heavy mast crops hold deer captive in the deep woods.) Whitetails find acorns, particularly those from sweet white oaks and related bur oaks, irresistible when they first fall to the ground. Many times I've observed deer rooting out acorns from beneath the leaves, hyperventilating like a broken vacuum. They get so intense that they sometimes make themselves nervous.

This is old hat to Jim Byford, an avid bowhunter and Dean of the School of Agriculture and Home Economics at the University of Tennessee at Martin. During a radio-tracking study, Byford proved that deer shift their home ranges in response to changing food supplies. A simple relationship unfolded: When food is concentrated, so are deer movements; when food is dispersed, deer movements are dispersed. "Although bucks temporarily forget about food during the rut," Byford says, "they still follow does who, in turn, key on fresh acorns to the exclusion of just about everything else."

Serious business! Here are a few canons to the acorn connection:

- When given the option, deer forsake day-old acorns for freshly cast ones. During a heavy mast year, the best way to tell which acorns are being targeted is by sniffing out deer droppings—literally. Fresh deer dung has a slight odor and is moist and pasty compared to older droppings, which become dry and fibrous. And don't forget color: Slick green is steaming fresh compared to dull brown or black droppings.

- A red oak's acorns are bitter compared to the mild, sweet taste of a white oak's. Deer turn to red oaks only after their supply of white-oak acorns has been depleted.

- Distinguish white from red oaks. Whereas white oaks flower and bear fruit every season, red oaks bear acorns every other year. This makes scouting red oaks for next year's hunt a snap, as the immature fruit is readily observed amongst the tops. In most areas, white oaks produce acorns first (usually beginning in September), followed by red oaks a couple of weeks to a month later. Finally, white oak leaves sport seven to nine rounded lobes; red-oak leaves are distinctly sharp and usually triple-pointed, with seven to 11 total lobes.

- Oaks on the top of a ridge will usually be the first to drop their acorns, and a steady progression follows for other oaks down the slope.

- Drought and early frost can lead to spotty acorn production (not bad for hunters, as it concentrates deer predictably in small pockets). In dry years, head for knolls facing north or northeast, where moisture retention is highest. Also, bur oaks are highly drought-resistant, preferring sandy soils. Higher elevations might be better than lower elevations when Old Man Winter pays an early visit.

- Oaks are easy to distinguish on aerial photos, thanks to their large, globular crowns. Sources for locating oak stands on public lands include the Forest Service, state forestry departments, county land or auditors' departments (administering tax-forfeited lands) and regional planning agencies. First look up the ownership on a plat map, then knock on the appropriate jurisdictional door. By the way, these officials are usually happy to introduce you to the aerial photo interpretation game.

- Don't hunt amidst the oaks but rather along a travel route—such as saddle between two ridges or knolls, the head of a hollow or natural lines of cover— where you can catch whitetails coming and going unawares. You will also spook less deer by hunting the fringes, and you can pick alternate routes for different winds.

When's the best time to hunt this nutty acorn connection? If nearby cover is plentiful, most any Moon time will do. Remember this when a Full or New Moon treats you to suppressed morning and evening deer activity. But if the oak stands are surrounded by a thin understory, you might need to hunt them like open croplands—along funnels where a buck can rack up for the day, sniffing does stepping out for a nutty treat.

If you do your homework and take these pointers to heart, you'll have a field day. ○

Chapter 5

THE SECOND STAGE: SOFT MASTS

stage (staj) \n\: "A center of attention or a place of rest."

I've been making a big deal about predicting when deer are most likely to be on their feet and heading for the kitchen. Although the rut's a great time to hunt, a whitetail's real Achilles' heel is its stomach (technically the microbes living in its rumen). Deer MUST eat. And they must eat regularly to survive, unlike predators feast-or-famine lifestyles. But knowing when deer must eat is not enough, and sometimes knowing "where" can be misleading.

This is a fair buck I arrowed near the edge of a field. For the real bruisers, you have to concentrate on staging areas.

I used to think, for example, that if I could figure out which crops -- clover, beans, alfalfa, oats, wheat, corn, milo -- the bucks were most interested in, I'd fill my tag within a few days. While the principles covering food sources and field edges in Chapter 4 are an excellent primer, there's a higher level to this proven system. It's time to reexamine the phenomenon of "staging." Only then can we fine-tune appropriate moon times for food-source hunts.

Though I've arrowed some respectable bucks by camping where field and woods meet, I shudder to think of the monsters I've been missing out on by failing to relocate a little deeper into the cover. We're talking the difference between whitetails grossing in the 130s and 140s versus those nearing the 160-or-better mark. It seems the bigger the rack, the more likely its owner will stage up.

Exactly where bucks stage used to be hit and miss. I relied mainly on buck sign to identify prime areas. When I stumbled onto a lot of extra-large "buck cakes" (droppings caked together like a small loaf of Italian bread), I knew right where the largest-bodied whitetails were spending a disproportionate amount of time; scattered rubs and nibbled browse often confirmed my hunch. Only problem was, many times I'd be a day or week late: By the time I arrived on the scene, the bucks would mysteriously switch to another staging area. As often as not I'd often find myself a step or two behind.

To get "there" before the bucks do, we need a deeper understanding of the dynamics of staging areas. I used to believe that bucks staged primarily to bide time, whiling away the day's remaining rays of light while eating alternative plant species until darkness.

Additionally, the more secluded a food source was, the more likely a buck would target it before dark. This is partly true. Bucks are better survivalists than does are, and can resist the urge to feed on vegetation until it's safe to do so. But, as the dictionary definition at the heading of this chapter implies, rest (safety) is only half the equation. Hunters can do a better job of identifying "centers of interest."

This is where soft mast comes in. Simply stated, key plant species falling within this category will consistently attract deer before and during hunting seasons, to the point that whitetail travel patterns become remarkably predictable. In other words, know the mast species of your respective region, and you'll know where most bucks will be staging up.

The real key to understanding food sources is knowing the difference between primary and secondary plant species.

Why Deer Eat What They Eat

We know that deer tend to feed most heavily during a moon time, but whitetails are notorious for dining on an exhaustive list of forbs, stems nuts, flowers, fruits, grains, and fungi: About 2,000 plant species have been documented in the rumen of whitetails. Further complicating matters is how deer often target one food item at the exclusion of all others, then switch seemingly overnight. In a practical way, deer are much like humans in that we both like variety. This is good because it ensures a balanced diet providing basic nutritional needs.

Recall the study at the Auburn Deer Research Facility, referenced in Chapter 4 Deer spent about the same amount of time feeding on volunteer "weeds" as they did on carefully planted forages. Dr. Keith Causey summed up his feelings this way:

"... I have devoted considerable time to researching the production, costs, deer preference and use of dozens of species and varieties of agronomic forages planted for white-tailed deer. There are numerous agronomic small grains and legumes that can produce an abundance of highly nutritious and palatable forage for deer if properly cultivated. However, it has been my observation over many years that white-tailed deer tend to use native foods, when available, more consistently than those that we plant for them."

When we add the fact that deer tend to choose a food source based on its relative convenience as much as its nutritional value and taste, we're one step closer to tapping one of the most illuminating hunting principles going: ALL DEER FOODS CAN BE SEGREGATED INTO PRIMARY AND SECONDARY SOURCES. The difference is literally night and day.

Bucks love the taste of soft mast, but it's also nutritious and convenient.

Daytime vs. Nocturnal Food

When researchers refer to a food's convenience, they're really saying that what's on the menu during daylight hours is radically different from what's available after dark. Given the whitetail's basic survival instinct of predator avoidance, where's the safest place to be after dark? Simple: Out in the open where light-gathering vision can be optimized, and at lower elevations where scent settles. Well, it just so happens that this is where lush vegetation is most prolific, thanks to an abundant supply of direct sunlight necessary for photosynthesis. No wonder deer like to load up on primary food species after dark.

Conversely, the safety first principle for daylight hours applies: Deer hang out in thick, shady cover because bright light inhibits their vision, and at higher elevations where thermals take scent for a daily ride to their noses. This is where secondary food sources thrive, often forcing deer to dine on woody browse and fibrous stems, twigs, and buds that are lower in crude protein. A notable exception is mast. This category of vegetation is not only rich in nutriments, but it's exceedingly palatable and almost always convenient.

Mast can be divided into two categories--hard and soft. Examples of hard mast are the ever-popular acorn and beechnut. Soft mast includes mainly fruits and berries, including common chokeberry, buffaloberry, serviceberry, common and western snowberry, bearberry, dogwood, muscadine grape and Panhandle grape, western soapberry, Chickasaw plum, common persimmon, honey mesquite mast, blackberry, yaupon, honey locust, coralberry, blackgum, dewberry, arrowwood viburnum, American beautyberry, dwarf palmetto, Chinaberry, and crabapple.

It pays to know your soft mast, in this case snowberry.

Coincidentally, deer dislike and avoid the following plant varieties (use them to safeguard your garden): barberry, scented geranium, ornamental grass, spruce, mint, catnip, goldenrod, thyme, and Adam's needle, to name a few.

Dead Deer Don't Lie

Anglers who want to know what fish are feeding on can simply open the viscera of their catch and find out in a matter of seconds without any guesswork. A similar tactic applies to hunters. Extensive stomach analysis research, conducted on thousands of road-killed whitetails over several decades in many parts of the nation, reveals just what deer prefer. Invariably, a handful of species show up in the rumens of deer time after time. For example, Harlow and Hooper analyzed the deer diet in the southern Appalachians by examining the rumen content of 298 whitetails. (The area includes parts of New York, Pennsylvania, Maryland, Virginia, Kentucky, Tennessee, Ohio, North and South Carolina, Georgia, Alabama, and West Virginia.) Oak mast was the most abundant food item in autumn, followed by Chinaberry, crabapple, persimmon, and grape, in

I arrowed this fine South Dakota Pope and Young whitetail in October by taking advantage of its stomach.

that order.

In coastal plains states (parts of Pennsylvania, Virginia, North and South Carolina, Georgia, Florida, Alabama, Mississippi, Louisiana, and Eastern Texas) researchers Murphy and Noble reported 81 species of plants utilized by bottom-land deer. And researcher Lay identified 69 plant species in East Texas, whereas Harlow found 193 food items in Florida deer. The highest quality deer foods tended to grow in bottomland hardwoods, and the lowest quality in loblolly and slash pine forests. Top species were, in order of preference, dwarf palmetto, American beautyberry, common persimmon, blackberry, Yaupon, dewberry, and arrowwood viburnum.

In the central and southern plains area (parts of Nebraska, Kansas, Oklahoma, eastern Colorado, and New Mexico) Mohler and associates found that 40 to 50 percent of deer forage consisted of farm crops, but as much as 21 percent included western snowberry in several states. Preferred shrubs included grape, common persimmon, western soapberry, Chickasaw plum, and American plum.

Texas Panhandle deer stomachs displayed the following preferences: Panhandle grape, western soapberry, Chickasaw plum, and common persimmon. In the Edwards Plateau 74 plants, seven shrubs, and 13 trees were utilized most often, with hackberry acorns topping the list; common persimmon, blackberry, yaupon, and greenbrier were close behind, and honey mesquite mast was significant where cattle overgrazed. Coincidentally, plains prickly pear comprised about 50 percent of the yearly diet in north-central Texas.

The northern Great Lakes states -- Minnesota, Wisconsin, and Michigan -- grow mostly wild berries that deer home in on: serviceberry, raspberry, black-berry, cherry, and hawthorn. And the Midwest oak/hickory forest (parts of Missouri, Illinois, Indiana, Ohio, Oklahoma, Arkansas, Mississippi, Tennessee, and Kentucky) is home to several key soft mast species, according to researcher Korschgen: coralberry, sumac, grapes, persimmon, and honey locust. Some additional variations: Tennessee deer preferred blackgum, strawberry bush, sumac, and grapes were important in the Ozarks, along with common poke-berry, rusty blackhaw viburnum, and blackberry.

Deer of the northern plains of North and South Dakota, Montana, Wyoming, and Nebraska prefer, in order of preference, common chokeberry, buffaloberry, service-berry, common snowberry, bearber-ry, and dogwood. South Dakota deer were especially fond of snow-

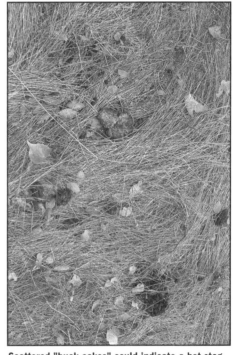

Scattered "buck cakes" could indicate a hot staging area.

48

berry, bearberry, and serviceberry, according to researcher Schneeweis.

Finally, in the Midwest agricultural region (parts of Minnesota, Iowa, Illinois, Kansas, Missouri, Indiana, and Ohio) crops made up 78 percent of food consumed by weight, 56 by volume, and 89 percent by occurrence, according to stomach analysis conducted by Mustard and Wright. But that doesn't mean soft mast won't play a major role in hunting plans.

Hard-core Tactics for Soft Mast

I recently rediscovered the significance of natural feeding cycles of whitetails. Professional tournament angler Mike McClelland leased the hunting rights to some cattle country in his home state of South Dakota, and he wanted my frank opinion of the resource's potential. It was good news, bad news. The good news was that the parcel -- 14 miles of creek bottom -- hadn't been hunted in a few years. The bad news was that there were no croplands whatsoever, and that the cattle had grazed down what little the ground could produce.

It soon became evident that most deer were bedding in the brushy creek bottom, but cutting them off as they headed for a particular food source was as frustrating as removing a cactus splinter without my reading glasses (I did this a lot on this trip). Seems each day the deer would come and go from a different quadrant as they fed on a multitude of native prairie species. But I got even when I noticed that a particular clump of berried bushes attracted a disproportionate number of deer. It's a long story, save to say I managed to hide in a small clump of trees and arrow a fine Pope and Young buck slipping out for an evening snack under an overhead moon. As I write this, McClelland is busy implementing a full-meal-deal habitat improvement program, replete with perennials (alfalfa) and natural mast preservation (acorns and prairie plants). For more information, contact Cheyenne Ridge Outfitters (800-223-9126; www.cheyenneridge.com).

To make the most of mast, first learn to identify specific food items that deer turn to year after year. Alpha does will lock onto a particular food item and pass that "information" on to succeeding generations. The following text provides a basic narrative on key mast species, and local county extension agents and university horticulturists can help put the finishing touches on a hunting strategy that makes biological sense. A good way to identify what some various deer foods look like is to visit the following web sites:

www.dcnr.state.pa.us/forestry/commontr/common.htm

As you draw up game plans, consider the Least Factor, coined by outdoorwriter Tim Jones several years ago: Food sources that are least available will be most desirable. A good base line strategy is mapping out micro pockets of soft mast that are sure to be visited when they ripen; orchestrate an efficient "milk run" from spot to spot; and check them often to make sure the resource is still available.

A case in point is a vacation homestead where my friend Gerry Bethge spends a lot of time during the deer season. About 15 years ago Bethge edited Outdoor Life magazine and authored a story on hunting deer over apples. "I was just learning about [the deer-apple connection] back then," he confessed, "but now I think I know the score. Besides location, the main key is timing. Deer will ignore apples, visiting them only occasionally throughout early fall, then go on a binge and wipe them out. I mean, one day the apples look like they'll rot away, the next day they're gone." The answer to this riddle is how the fermentation process of frost activity "sweetens" apples to the liking of deer. In fact, fermentation affects the palatability of many fruit and berry species--whitetails know exactly when this occurs and are efficient opportunists.

Naturally, scouting plays a significant role in practical hunting strategies revolving around soft mast. Some legwork will be necessary, but here's a surefire shortcut: Identify the flowers of local mast species. Why flowers? Because they stand out from a distance! I conduct a lot of "flower power" reconnaissance during spring turkey seasons, plotting precise locations with a hand-held GPS on a topo map. Then I can quickly find choice, out-of-the-way thickets to return to when the fruits are due to ripen.

By all means incorporate soft mast with food plot- and crop-land-based tactics.

Got apples? Then you've got deer.

Recall the Midwest study with 89 percent of deer stomachs (by volume) containing croplands. Deer in the agricultural belt don't just lie in their beds till sunset, then make a beeline for farm crops. A few might, such as does entering the final days of their estrus cycle, but the majority of bucks will stage up and master on mast. Fact is, given a choice bucks will target succulent soft mast over bitter browse and bland forbs and grasses every time. Translation: Set up treestands and ground blinds downwind of ripe soft mast species situated between croplands and security cover.

Food plots and cultivated croplands certainly play a significant role in maintaining robust whitetail herds. And field-edge game plans are an obliging tactic for outwitting whitetails. But if you want to graduate from middling bucks to studs that demand a double-take, you'll bone up on natural foods that whitetails find irresistible.

MASTERING SOFT MAST

"Mast" is a general term referring to the reproductive bodies of plants, particularly wildlife plant species. Technically, "soft mast" describes seeds that are covered with fleshy fruit, such as apples and berries; however, soft mast may also include the seeds and fruits of grasses, herbs (forbs), pines, and even fungi. Below is a brief description of the North America's leading soft mast species; there are four major species, about a dozen minor ones.

CRABAPPLE The trees are deciduous, usually thorny, and generally less than 30 feet tall. The golf-ball-size fruit matures between August and November, depending on variety and geography. Color varies from green-yellow to red, and mature fruit drops to the ground shortly after ripening. Crabapple trees "like" to grow in thickets, making Considerable concentrations available in relatively small areas. Abundant fruit crops generally occur about every two to four years. Incidentally, abandoned orchards on old homestead sites may produce enough fruit to attract predictable whitetail visitations. Planting crabapples should be a part of every comprehensive habitat strategy. The following crabapple species are superior tasting and scab-resistant: Ralph Shay, Centurion, Profusion, Adams.

COMMON PERSIMMON This small- to medium-sized deciduous tree grows in open woods, old fields, and edges from Connecticut to southern Ohio, from Kansas to as far south as Florida and Texas. In rich bottomlands tree height can scale 80 feet with trunk diameters of two or more feet. The plum-like fruit, three-quarters to two inches in diameter, is green before ripening and notably astringent; however, when thoroughly ripe it's sweet and enjoyed by humans. Maturation varies from September to November, and the fruit can be green, yellow, orange, yellowish brown, dark red, purple, and even black. Prolific fruit crops occur about every two years with light crops in alternate years. Only female trees bear fruits.

WILD GRAPES The muscadine wild grape is generally the most attractive species to whitetails. Range is moist soils from Delaware to Kentucky and Missouri, south to Texas and eastward to Florida. Muscadine is a climbing vine that can be identified by its tight, non-shredding bark. Toothed leaves are less deeply lobed than other wild grapes, and the leaves are generally round. Fruit size ranges from dime- to quarter-size at maturity. They are green before ripening into a golden bronze or deep purple. Bowhunters have the best odds on muscadines which ripen in late-summer to early fall (July to September).

HONEY LOCUST This tree grows as tall as 150 feet but individuals this size are limited to rich bottomlands and limestone soils in the eastern U.S. (except New England and the south Atlantic and coastal plains). Deer dine heavily on the seed pods (eight to 18 inches long, about one inch wide) of this member of the bean family. Ripe pods are varied hues of brown and look like a twisted, flattened banana. Experts are divided on exactly what deer are attracted to, but the general consensus is that the sweet pulp inside the pod is more desirable than the seeds. Production varies from year to year and tree to tree. Water locust and the hybrid Texas honey locust are not as sweet. Scouting for the "honey" content of the best trees is easy -- taste and see for yourself. Highest pod production comes from trees older than 25 years, and the best crops are produced every other year or two, although a few trees bear fruit annually.

The following "minor" mast species are often found in enough abundance to help hunters pattern whitetail deer movements:

JAPANESE HONEYSUCKLE This twisting, twining woody vine of the South and East enwraps bushes and climbs tall trees. It produces highly fragrant, double-pilled flowers (white to pink when young; yellow with age). The fruit is multi-seeded, black and pulpy, maturing in early autumn. The controversial Japanese honeysuckle has spread like weeds since it was first imported from Asia to Long Island in 1862; native species include the trumpet and wild honeysuckle. Deer browse on the vines and use the shade of the spreading honeysuckle for concealment. Enterprising hunters in the South can pattern deer exclusively by observing the progression of honeysuckle development.

BUFFALOBERRY With its silvery leaves and scarlet fruit, this shrub grows on the prairies of Alberta, Manitoba, and Saskatchewan. Commonly found around sloughs and in coulees, the silver buffaloberry is a large, thorny shrub with multiple branches. The yellow flowers are inconspicuous at a distance. Fruit is reddish orange about a quarter-inch in diameter and develops in August to September. The berries are quite sour, but a hard frost improves taste--and the number of deer visitations.

SERVICEBERRY Some species occur over most parts of the United States, and they produce edible fruits. Most are shrubs or small trees, up to 20 feet, but typically smaller. The fruits are produced in small open clusters known as racemes. Individual fruits are less than one-third-inch in diameter and are black and round. When ripe, they are sweet enough to be eaten fresh or used in pies and jams.

SNOWBERRY is the common name for a bushy American shrub belonging to the family Caprifoliaceae (see honeysuckle). The snowberry is known for its loose, leafy cluster of snow-white berries at the ends of the branches.

BEARBERRY A small shrub with heavily branched, irregularly stemmed evergreen leaves, the bearberry is most abundant in northern latitudes The half-inch-long evergreen leaves possess a leathery texture, are rounded at the apex, and taper gradually toward the base to a short stalk. The bright-red berries (the size of small currants) are smooth and shiny and ripen in the fall. Inside the tough skin is a drab, mealy pulp with a handful of stony seeds.

SOAPBERRY This tree grows to about 35 feet, has white flowers in the spring, and ranges as far south as the Texas Hill Country and western Florida. When the soapberry loses its leaves in winter, its marble-sized translucent/amber fruit reveals tiny black seeds inside. The fruit tends to hang onto the tree throughout the winter. This species tolerates a wide range of soils, including dry, stony, and nutrient-deficient classifications.

YAUPON A shrubby small tree with leathery, dark-green evergreen leaves and bright-red berries, Yaupon often grows in dense clumps. The bark is smooth and gray and may be mottled yellow-green. Flowers are inconspicuous. Yaupon inhabits well-drained areas along the southeastern United States coastal plain -- from southern Virginia to central Florida and as far west as Texas, Oklahoma, and Arkansas.

AMERICAN BEAUTYBERRY This shrub is important to many wildlife species not only because of its purple fruit, but because of its drought-resistance nature. Look for purple blossoms that bloom in the fall.

VIBURNUM This popular deciduous garden shrub grows in the wild, yields flowers and fruits, and has 120 species in the genus (belonging to the honeysuckle family). While some varieties grow best in direct sunlight, most will grow and flower in the shade. The pulpy fruit contains one or more stony seeds; the berry, or "drupe," may be yellow, red, blue, or black.

CHINABERRY The shade-intolerant chinaberry has naturalized itself in open areas throughout the Southeast. Identify it by its alternate leaves that are toothed-to-lobed leaflets. Twigs are stout, maroon, and shiny with no terminal bud; the bark is purple-maroon and shiny on young stems and brown and ridged on larger trees. Flowers are purple and showy; fruit is a yellow-brown poisonous drupe.

DWARF PALMETTO This trunkless, sharp-bladed "fan" bush is exceedingly drought-resistant and prefers sunny areas over shade. The palmetto is restricted to the Southeast. Its fruit is black when ripe (one-half inch) and the seeds are glossy dark red or brown.

CHICKASAW PLUM This shrub grows in clonal thickets and may be as tall as eight feet. The bark is red-brown to dark gray with thin scales; wigs are lustrous red-brown; the white flowers appear from March to April; and the fruit drupes mature from May to July. Use the chickasaw plum to identify bachelor groups of bucks that dine heavily at times on the lush red fruits.

DEWBERRY is a common name for several varieties of blackberry, but the dewberry differs from other types by its long, slender stems that trail along the ground. The western dewberry varieties are also trailing, and hybridization produces the loganberry, youngberry and boysenberry. O

Chapter 6

TIMING THE TRANSITION ZONE

tran·si·tion (tran-zi-shŏn): "Passage from one condition or area to another."

A couple years ago, my friend Tim Anick was asked to stop at the grocery store on the way home from work. His fiancee needed some corned beef and hash browns. Imagine the look on Tracy's face when Tim retrieved two cans of corned beef hash from his grocery bag! I still chuckle when I think of this blooper, especially when I hear some hunters trying to explain transition-zone hunting. They sound like they know what they're talking about, but I wonder. Good communication can prevent long-cuts, so let's first come to terms with transition Moon times: Think midmorning and midafternoon. A Moon time anywhere from sunrise to 10 a.m. and again two or three hours before dark presents an excellent opportunity to waylay a buck in the in-between zone.

Operation Interception

My fondest whitetail memory in recent years is a Nebraska bowhunt during which my partner Gayle Verbeck spotted a big buck steal past him just out of range on the September opener. I ended up arrowing the 150-class Pope and Young buck on the last day of my hunt by using the Moon's influence to intercept the buck between a food plot and a distant willow thicket bordering the Platte River.

The key word for transition hunting is interception. As explained in Chapter 2, the Deer Hunters' Moon Guide™ system separates deer activity into three basic areas, of which the transition zone is merely a lane of travel and not a destination. It also happens to be Myles Keller's most productive area year in and year out.

"Before the season, bowhunters talk a good talk," Myles says. "They all seem to agree that once a buck knows he's being hunted, he becomes nearly unkillable. Hunters say the buck goes nocturnal, if they see buck sign but not the buck; but I don't think this is the case that often. From my experiences it's obvious the buck is simply beating the hunter.

"Why? Because when a hunter moves too close to a bedding area, he usually disturbs the buck. If bowhunters really believe what they say, they'd avoid a cat-and-mouse game, replacing it with strategies designed to catch the buck totally off-guard."

According to Myles, the transition zone is made to order for this. "Apart from a few glaring exceptions, hunting so-called rutting areas isn't nearly as productive as outdoor magazines make it out to be. To begin with, most scrape activity is nocturnal in nature. And a buck entering this turf is on edge as he contends with

55

rival bucks when he searches for receptive does. His senses are working overtime. You might see some middle-aged bucks here, but you won't get many shots at the area's dominant breeders. They'll usually figure you out first.

"However, you can reverse this trend by hanging back, biding your time, catching the buck traveling between feeding and bedding areas. Figure where the buck has to come from to scent-check his scrapes for does coming into heat. Or find out where he heads after he checks them out. To have a fighting chance, I want to hunt a buck that's as relaxed as he's ever going to get, maybe even a bit lazy. Then he's more likely to cut a corner, make a little mistake. This is far superior to wading into a buck's backyard, dueling with him on his own terms. My strategy has worked for me so many times… I see no reason to change it."

This is a good place to explain two key ingredients of Myles' system. He's written the book on scent-control, enjoying a profitable relationship with Robinson Laboratories (Scent Shield products). But he also takes concealment very seriously. At one time during his career he tie-dyed his own camouflage pattern because he didn't like the way existing patterns on the market blended together.

I arrowed this fine Nebraska eight-pointer with matching sticker points in a classic transitional area; the in-between zone is ideally suited for down 'n' dirty bowhunting.

"They may look nice on a clothing rack," he said. "But they'll give you away if a buck ever scans the horizon. Your outline must be broken up completely." Until recently, Myles didn't think the ideal camo pattern existed. He liked how Predator appeared at a distance, and he liked other patterns for the way they looked up close. Then along came Advantage (a division of Spartan Realtree). "I fell in love with the design right away. It has a unique combination that's plenty busy—with branches and leaves and such—but not so detailed that it blends together into a blob from afar. It's also got a chameleon-like effect the way it responds to both dim and strong light."

Myles has a definite Advantage when it comes to camouflage.

The Glass Eye

When you go scout-hunting for these areas, don't forget your binoculars. Western hunters never leave camp without quality optics, and deer hunters who fail to take advantage of them are severely handicapping themselves. My binoculars give me a visual edge to the same degree that a whitetail's nose gives him a powerful olfactory system. From a distance, I can study deer that don't have a clue I'm on the same planet, let alone in the same county.

Earlier I mentioned "low-light optics." If you don't invest wisely, you'll be disappointed when light is at a premium. To avoid an optical illusion, here's what to look for.

- The specifications to which binoculars are made affect their light transmission as much as the quality of their components. Briefly, the larger the front objective lens, the more light it collects; and the greater the power, or magnification, the lower its brightness. Thus, a moderately priced 7 x 50 binocular (which magnifies an object seven times and has a front lens measuring 50 mm in diameter) will be noticeably brighter during twilight than a pricey 8 x 30.
- The exit-pupil diameter—the size of the tiny circles of light you see in the binocular's eyepiece when you hold it at arms' length—demands attention. The human eye dilates from approximately 2mm (during bright light) to 7mm (after sunset). This explains why an entry-level 7 x 35 binocular may be as effective during midday as a premium 7 x 50. When light is low, however, a binocular with an exit pupil properly matched to a fully dilated human pupil will really shine.

Determine exit-pupil diameter with a simple math equation: divide the objective lens diameter by the magnification: for 7 x 35 binoculars, 35 ÷ 7 = 5 exit pupil; 8 x 40 = 5 exit pupil; 7 x 50 = 7.1 exit pupil etc. Unfortunately, to get much above an exit pupil of 5mm, the bulk and weight of the optics becomes excessive. Enterprising hunters glass with 7 x 50s from their vehicles, switching to shirtpocket models when retreating to the hinterlands. The bottom line: Match magnification with objective-lens diameter to achieve an exit pupil of at least 5 (4 is acceptable in pocket models). Incidentally, spotting scopes, with their dramatic magnification, must be compromised: 3 is the minimum exit pupil.

An optic's efficiency also determines its performance under demanding low-light conditions.

- Transmitted brightness—how much light actually reaches your eye—is affected by the quality of the optics. Eighty percent is generally considered good to excellent and 90 percent is simply eye-popping (but cost-prohibitive for most).

The 7x50 binocular in my left hand is perfect for glassing from the truck... but I wouldn't want it bouncing off my chest all day as I scout on foot.

- To attain the maximum brightness, purchase only optics that are "fully coated" or "fully multi-coated." Plain "coated" won't do.

- Roof prism optics are more compact but rarely as sharp as porro prism models. (You can tell the difference by shape—the former is streamlined, the latter's eyepieces are offset from the objective lenses.) The only exception to this rule involves high-priced models with a phase-correction coating.

- Compare and contrast prices, but a simple side-by-side trial is the ultimate test. When I propped up a pair of Bausch & Lomb 7 x 26 Custom Compacts, then tested an overseas big-name, big-price tag model, I settled on the Bausch & Lombs. An extra $200 for the foreign glasses didn't deliver $200 more of light. By the way, be sure to conduct your test during the in-between period of twilight.

Now you're ready to pick the right vantage point—one that not only gives you a good feel for general deer movements, but one that just might give you a shot at a nice buck. From one of his many "observation stands" along a fenceline or treeline, Myles learns a lot more than he would hunting over a rub line or scrape line. He also learns when to make his next move.

A spell of scout-hunting should help you exploit a buck's peculiar weakness—one that only shows up, however, when he's gotten into a routine uninhibited by man's intrusion into his domain.

"Apart from the dead of the rut [at night], no respectable buck will ever put himself in a totally compromising position," Myles says. "For example, if the wind's perfect for you, it's useless for the buck; he knows it, and you're wasting your time in that arrangement. But if the wind's slightly quartering, at certain times in certain situations the buck will cut across it, relying mostly on his eyes and not on his nose."

A case in point is a Pope and Young buck Myles arrowed a few years ago that taught him to "split the difference" on wind direction. The studious bowhunter glassed a dandy 10-pointer several mornings in a row. Each time the buck followed the edge of an east/west drainage ditch and then cut across the wind for about 100 yards before diving into a woodlot to the north. Myles slipped in from the back side of the security cover and intercepted the buck at the only juncture where the trophy couldn't use the wind.

This is a universal morning strategy, according to Myles. "It seems to work best when bucks have been feeding or chasing does in the wee hours of the night and into the morning. When they suddenly realize the sun's against them, they're anxious to make it to security cover. So they cut across the wind to save time. They'll never do this, however, if they've picked up any human scent near the area."

This is how Myles hunts the "connecting cover" of draws, creekbottoms, ravines, fencelines, treelines—any logical travel route a buck likes to follow as he travels to and fro. Invariably, Myles cuts no corners when setting up where a buck is likely to cut cross-wind. These "areas of compromise" are a critical part of the transition-zone package. You must wait for the wind to be just so…

Best Buck Ever

Myles has arrowed a lot of record-book bucks, including several in the 160s and a dandy Wisconsin eight-pointer measuring 175 5/8. But his best-ever, a Manitoba monster scoring 185 Boone and Crockett points that he took on November 2, 1994, is yet another example of what the transition zone can cough up… if you hunt it the way Myles does.

"Bucks and food sources are a legitimate combination if hunting pressure is under control," he said. "But even if the pressure is light, it's hard to pick a buck off right on the edge of the field. Even when they see other deer out there chowing down, something seems to tell them to hold back. Increased pressure, with hunters educating bucks daily to the dangers of open areas, has definitely taken its toll. Early in my career I arrowed a lot of nice bucks near fields, but not many since.

"On my Manitoba trip, I caught a glimpse of a good buck in the distance while walking to an area I wanted to check out. I decided to hang way back and hopefully intercept him in transition cover before he got to the area. I ended up not getting to him in the first spot because I thought it was a touchy bedding area, and he was outside of his main routine. Then I decided to drive home when nothing was moving and return a week or so later when I could put two and two together.

"[When I got back] right away I saw the huge tracks. I like to gauge a buck by his stride more than by the size of his spoors. The first thing I check is whether the hind prints overstep the front ones—an outstanding buck is longer, stiffer, and his back legs don't get very close to his front legs. It's so easy to spot in his trail.

"So now I know there's a good buck traveling between and around two patches of bush near a field; I know where the deer are bedding from this intersection; and I know that in the corner of one of the thickets there's a small opening where I can shoot out into the field and also monitor the middle of the cover. But, as is often the case, trying to cover too much ground with a bow usually leads to nothing… so this setup was actually an exception to my normal hunting style. I watched for two days from the ground because the trees were too

Myles and his best-ever 185 Boone and Crockett buck. Are you missing out by not capitalizing on the transition zone?

small and would have certainly given me away.

"Next, I decided to circle clear around, ford a creek and relocate where I could enter from the backside. I hung a treestand when I was sure the deer were tucked back in their beds, and got the heck out of there. Well, the next morning, about 8:30 or 9, a bunch of deer came right through, cutting my track—which I never want to happen, especially with snow on the ground, but I had to make a loop to get in there. The deer came through in front of me, anyway, including one that would have made minimum. I let them pass, but the big boy doesn't show. As they romp out of sight I catch the wide, tall rack I'd been looking for. It was a longer-than-normal shot for me, but I've gained a lot of confidence in my Xi bow, and I knew the extra speed would some day come in handy."

After the ambrosia of another rewarding hunt began to fade, Myles realized he needed to do some investigating. "The buck should have been with the other deer, and it began to eat away at me," he said. "So I backtracked his trail. I learned once again what bowhunters are up against when a big buck goes on the defensive: He made a point to circle the funnel, even though his sentinels had passed through safely, apparently because he had cut my tracks back by the creek. Instead of following the other deer, he entered the other chunk of bush, hit the open field, then took up their trail on the other side. I was very fortunate to tag that monster—the biggest buck of my life didn't get away."

Why didn't Myles locate at the edge of the bedding area and catch the buck at the back door? Sometimes you have to, but it's a tough game. All too often the buck circles downwind, licking the currents all the way in. He'll pick you up if you don't have an extraordinary setup. Better to use the Moon's influence on deer when it tells them to linger near food sources longer than usual during the morning hours.

Line up an early to midmorning Moon time with an appropriate "area of compromise," and you're in the right place at the right time.

"The tremendous advantage of hunting around the Moon is that hunters can predict their best shot well in advance," Myles says. "You don't have to waste time in a morning-only spot or wait for deer that aren't going to show up in the evening. Bowhunters just don't get it that a big whitetail will adapt to everything hunters throw at him. Once he's onto you, he's almost unkillable; his survival instinct overpowers his need to eat and mate. But the Moon can help a guy pick the best time to work-over a good buck—I mean do it seriously and do it right. Most guys go out when things aren't happening, ding around and blow it. The Deer Hunters' Moon Guide™ system of rotating stands in line with the Moon is the most accurate and advanced explanation of how the lunar cycle affects hunting."

Get To The Point

Myles spends most fall days in transition lands—where wooded tracts are broken up by agricultural operations—but the same basic rules apply to forested regions of North America. The main difference is that deer travel is less concentrated. To boost the odds, hunters must discern key features that funnel game predictably. Here's how my poet friend Dave Peterson sees it:

The Moon's overhead in the morning sky,
The deer are on the move, and so am I.
I'll be threading my way to that bottleneck bluff,
Where trails converge, and the going gets tough.

Got another funnel of which I'm fond,
For a different wind, it's behind the pond.
There's no denying the deer will show,
Where I'll be hiding with my bow.

The Moon tells me the time is prime,
To bag my buck around breakfast time.
"These deer will be movin'," says the Lunar Guy,
"When I'm directly overhead in the early sky."

A tip of high ground jutting into a swamp—or poking into an acorn-bearing oak stand or cutting a CRP patch in two—is an excellent intercepting point. When a buck reaches the end of a ridge, he has to make a decision. Should he curve around the point or dive into the bottomland? Bank down the hill and skirt the edge of cover… or loop back? As he considers his options, he'll likely hit the skids at the very tip of the point. Finding a hot deer crossing is nice, but locating one that affords an open, unhurried shot like this is what every hunter dreams of. Get to the point, and you can have both.

Hunting points proficiently takes forethought and a measure of discipline. Topping the list of requirements is getting there without spooking deer. Too many hunters trudge through surrounding lowland in the dark by flashlight, literally blowing deer out of their hunting area. Instead, use your overlay map to plan routes that get you near the top of the ridge or knoll in a hurry, then straddle the ridge on the opposite side you intend to hunt. (Always stay below the horizon.)

This deep woods buck of mine is a pointed reminder of a certain tip of a popple ridge.

Of course, there's more to hunting a point than settling on the edge of the slope. You've got to learn the ins and outs of lowland and highland points, as well as the subtleties of single and multiple points. In addition, key variables such as wind eddies, benches and saddles must be considered.

Following are some pointers for lowland points and ridges:

- They rarely rise more than 50 feet, so up-and-down travel isn't constricting to deer; however, points broken up by a short section of swamp can be killers, as bucks take the shortest route between two sections of cover.
- Fingers poking into the bottoms bump the odds, because most have intersecting trails—one running down the hill into the bottomland, another paralleling the ridge, typically at the base. Sometimes you'll find so many trails that "the deer have passing lanes," as my friend Charlie Fig once quipped.
- Consider cover transitions. Aldo Leopold, a forefather of the science of wildlife management, noted that "game is a phenomenon of edges… occurring where the types of food and cover which it needs come together." Indeed, deer habitually skirt the seam where pine meets aspen, clear-cut kisses old growth, second growth hits sucker growth, and so on.
- A unique configuration that attracts bedded deer is a swamp downwind from a horseshoe-shaped ridge. With this layout, a buck can hear and see danger from the swamp while continually tasting winds at his backside. Moreover, the U-shaped contours deflect wind currents in several directions simultaneously.

The game is the same for highland points, but some rules change with the rise in elevation (ridges topping out 100 feet or more). Deer, like humans, take predictable paths of least resistance. Travel habits emerge:

- Most highland points have two or three main trails—one on the top and one or two along the sidehill. Follow these trails until they merge with secondary trails. The key spot is usually at the end of the point, where a pair of sidehill trails intersects.
- Oak-studded fingers, especially those nosing into lowland security cover, can be hot all day, all fall. When the acorns disappear, rutting activity commences, because the does will be bedding a short distance away.
- Converging points—where two or more ridges meet—often form a neat tic-tac-toe grid of trails as sidehill trails hook up with ridgetop byways.
- When the heat is on, key on a pressure point: Deer cut across saddles, or dips along the ridgeline, that are more easily negotiated than nearby steeper slopes. You may not find much deer sign here because most deer parallel the steep slopes. But if the cover is to a buck's liking, he'll mosey up the slope, possibly browsing along the way, and perhaps bed just over the top on the other side. Again, scent from every direction collects right under his nose.
- Plot out benches (flat stair-steps) that collect deer during the rut, if they're open but not too open. You have to strain to read the deer sign on these high-percentage, seemingly low-impact areas—deer nibbling on forbs chew them to the very root and this makes it look like there's nothing to eat. Bend down at deer level or look a little higher for regrowth on browse (a tip-off is a tiny "Y" at the tip).
- Ridgetop trails, with their inviting rubs, scrapes and grooved runways, are deceiving. Deer are skylined against a naked backdrop, and they seem to sense it. Consequently, most ridgetop trails are nighttime highways but day-time dead-ends.

These pointers must be negotiated with tricky winds in mind. Before you gallop for the nearest saddle—or park your fanny on the best-looking bench—learn to play wind currents like an osprey. Back-drafts billow when a gust of wind spirals over the hilltop, swirling down the gully. Ontario logger Bill Lankinen makes a science out of hunting swirling winds: He mainly avoids them. If the Man in the Moon graces you with a favorable transitional Moon time on your next day off, take some advice from Lankinen and hunt only dead-calm conditions at mid-morning.

"As morning thermals build, they should pull your scent up the hill," Lankinen says. "But the instant the wind stirs, you've got to move across the hill. Updrafting is inevitable when the thermals mix with prevailing winds." This makes stillhunting and ground blinds top bets for whitetails on ridges.

Bill Barkley has arrowed a handful of bucks by stillhunting points. "If the ground has any moisture, sneaking beats stand-hunting 10 to one," he says. "The secret is hunting a ridge that splits a quartering wind. You've got the deer hemmed in. If they try circling, just double-back; you know exactly where they're headed."

Barkley arrives at a favorite ridge about a half-hour before sunrise. After monitoring the downwind point for the first hour or so, he slinks along sidehill trails that are usually about a third of the way below the hilltop. He may pause up to 20 minutes at strategic locations as he pans the landscape with his binoculars. This is essential when hardwood leaves are curled and brittle.

Bill Lankinen kills most of his deer by tracking them when Moon times are most favorable, which is usually midmorning. Like Larry Weishuhn, Lankinen would much rather go one on one with a buck that's on his feet than one that's curled up in his bed. "I can get right on top of a buck when he's browsing, eh," Lankinen says. "I can tell from the meandering tracks and nipped branches he's filling his stomach and not paying attention to his backtrack. The Moon tells me when I've got the odds on my side… or if I have to try a different strategy." This refined method is how Lankinen killed four of his biggest bucks, all Boone and Crockett-class animals.

Blind Luck

Myles Keller's fine-tuned hunting system isn't about to change overnight—with the exception of one glaring detail. That 185-point Booner, discussed earlier, taught Myles a particularly memorable lesson. "For years I've wasted too much time hanging and unhanging portable treestands," he says. "From now on I'll be hunting more from the ground now that I've gotten over the stigma. Portable blinds are super-effective."

A fistful of reasons tell me hunting from the ground is frequently more effective than from an elevated perch. First, finding a decent tree exactly where you want it is hardly a given—often it's either too close or too far from game trails and hot sign. Second, in the time it takes to spell f-i-c-k-l-e, a wind shift can render an ideal tree location useless. Third, hunting from above can be a chilling experience, as brisk winds add real meaning to the word windchill. Fourth, expeditious stand relocation is impractical, if not impossible, in many situations because of the ruckus it makes in the woods. And fifth, scrambling nimbly and noiselessly down a tree—and back up another one—is a major undertaking (and semi-dangerous) for some hunters.

On the other hand, hunting from the ground can be kick-back comfortable. John Hambleton, a successful Iowa outfitter with five Pope and Young bucks to his credit—all taken from the ground—has no qualms about "grounding" his clients.

"You can pour a cup of hot soup, stretch your legs and really dig in without deer noticing," Hambleton says. "But up in a tree, you're naked. In most trees, deer pick out your skylined or silhouetted movements no matter how high you go." Hambleton might be right when he claims treestanders' movements are responsible for spooking more deer than human scent, because deer have become increasingly educated to danger from above.

In some habitats, hunting from the ground increases visibility. In conifers, for example, you can see better looking under pine boughs rather than through or over them. This principle stands water in mature forests with a thin understory.

The chief advantage of ground blinds is mobility. For example, it's no big deal heading off deer that manage to slip by out of range. One time a buddy noticed a glint of sunlight reflecting off an antler tine in the distance. The enterprising bowhunter waited for the buck to feed out of view, then circled around a knoll to cut him off. Try pulling this off from a treestand. By the time you've let the deer wander out of view, it'll be too far away to intercept.

The Ground Rules

There's no denying a ground blind has its share of limitations. Scent control and concealment top the list when hunting eye-to-eye with deer. Follow these

If you want to change your luck, learn how to blind-side a buck.

simple rules, however, and you might wonder why you risk life and limb on high:

• Pre-planning is the only antidote for fickle winds. Suppose a hot deer trail connects a midday bedding area with an evening feeding area. Plan alternative sites for contrary winds rather than get caught with a wind shift and have to improvise at the last minute.

• When hunting hilly terrain, don't forget thermals. Situate blinds on the uphill side of trails for morning hunts and below them for late-afternoon vigils. The exception is dark, dank overcast days during which the sun is blocked from warming up mother Earth.

• Bottomlands—creeks, deep draws, valleys—can be just as temperamental: Swirling winds bend and shape back-drafts capable of eddying human scent in four directions at the same time.

• Transcend all this by setting up where deer are forced to travel upwind. Dakota bowhunter Dennis Howell erects a ground blind behind a life-size buck decoy, with the Missouri River at his back. "I've had deer poke their noses into my blind without suspecting a thing," he told me. "One time a doe nibbled on one of the branches [fashioned together] while I held my breath for the trailing buck to draw near."

Other topographical barriers—from open fields to foreboding bogs, from large lakes to small beaver ponds—force deer around the edges, often causing them to compromise wind direction. Set up at the apex.

• As you deal with the wind, don't forget the sun. A minor nuisance to treestanders, bright sunlight is the kiss of death to ground-keepers. Aiming into a rising or setting sun is a complication to be avoided. As is setting up in the sun's direct rays which "don't exactly enhance camouflage patterns," Hambleton says. Again, lay out alternative ground-blind sites after studying where the sun casts shadows in relation to deer trails.

Field these grounders, too:

• The best companion in a natural blind is a small swivel seat. John Hambleton makes one of the best.

65

3-D ASAT camo is an effective pattern for hunting eye-to-eye in transition cover.

• Never pop up like a jack-in-the-box to shoot, unless deer are facing away or obstructed from your view.
• Consider rattling with a partner from a pair of ground blinds—one for the rattler, one for the rattlee.
• One of the best camo patterns for ground-pounding is 3-D ASAT.

It's The Pits

Borrow a page from the late Toad Smith, legendary Iowa sportsman, and dig yourself a pit blind. It seems the Toadster discovered a hotspot where deer habitually fed but where there was no way he could hide from their approaching view. The clever bowhunter rolled up his sleeves and dug himself a comfy pit. "It took me three years," he told me with a toothy grin. "Every time I passed through the area, I got out the shovel and subtracted another foot or two from the trench."

Needless to say, Smith arrowed Mr. Goodbuck from that blind on the fourth year.

The obvious pitfall with this strategy is that once you've dug your pit, you're in a hole—literally. Forget relocating. So dig a little deeper when scouting for potential pit blinds. Take your time like Smith did as you prospect dips in fields and old drainages that routinely attract deer, even during daylight hours. (Of course, the pits must be out of view of human traffic).

(A footnote: Dig the pit for easy eye-level view—remember the swivel stool—and add an extra foot of weeds or sticks to peek through.)

Whereas natural ground blinds hamstring you to one spot, a lightweight portable blind opens the door to some nifty footwork. For example, in the South and West, hunters have learned to call deer and elk from blinds, relocating positions throughout the day as necessary.

"You can cover a lot of ground from the ground with a portable," Hambleton says. "In unfamiliar territory, ground-pounding lets you hunt with a low profile as you scout."

Now, that sounds familiar. Being grounded isn't such a bad thing... unless you're a teenager.

In sum, the transition zone is the most consistent producer of big game. About one-third of the lunar cycle ensures activity along these corridors early to mid-morning and again in late-afternoon. Moderate traffic and a hunter-friendly habitat combine to make the in-between zone the best of both worlds. ○

Can't Find A Blind?

Commercial blinds have never looked so good:

- Build a blind to your specifications with a roll of nylon or burlap "camouflage netting." Hunter's Specialties, 6000 Huntington Court N.E., Cedar Rapids, IA 52402. 319-395-0321.

- The very best portable blind I've had the privilege of hunting out of is Double Bull Archery's ICE series (PO Box 923,1401-B Fallon, Monticello, MN 55362; 888-464-0409). This design goes up in seconds, not minutes, and is eminently portable at about 7 pounds. Naturally it's windproof and practically waterproof, confining your scent to the inner walls if you open only the "silent windows" you're peering out of. By the way, Double Bull also offers comfy portable seats with a back-saving back rest.

Double Bull Archery's portable blinds go up in seconds, not minutes,

- John Hambleton's Porta-Stump bears a remarkable resemblance to, well, a stump. His Tote Stool hooks conveniently on a belt, pivots quietly 360 degrees and spikes easily into the ground. P.S. Mfg. Co., 2462 160th Road, Guthrie Center, IA 50115. 800-695-8012.

Chapter 7

HOW & WHEN TO HUNT BEDDED BUCKS

The Moon's overhead in the middle of the day,
And you can bet the bedded buck is tucked away.
In the underbrush of his moated castle,
Safe, he thinks, from the hunter's hassle.

But I'm downwind knocking at his residence,
No noise, no scents, it all makes sense.
Well, he can't escape today, hiding midday,
Not since the Moon taught me the ungulate way.

There'll be no rest for this 10-point buck,
Except in the bed of my pickup truck.
Listening to the Moon is my ticket,
"For a noontime Moon Time, try the thicket."

Hunting when deer don't seem to be on the move is like throwing B'rer Rabbit in the briar patch: A foxy predator eventually learns the tables are turned. And so it is during most Full and New Moon periods of the lunar cycle. In a moment I'll explore the best options when deer seem to vanish. But first, we need to know what we're up against.

When the Moon peaks anywhere from 10:30 a.m. to 2:30 p.m., where will deer be? Most likely curled up in their beds. Percentage-wise, this time frame encompasses two-thirds of the lunar cycle, and it's the principal reason we don't see much game most days afield (and why we seem to see the majority of game on a handful of days). Midday Moon times find deer back in the thick stuff, and bucks just won't stray far to feed when daylight is strongest. The way the Creator fashioned the eyes of ungulates all but guarantees this.

Insights To Ungulates

Dr. Jay Neitz is a vision scientist who conducted post-doctoral work at the University of California. He examined the eye of ungulates (in this case, pigs), comparing them to those of humans. The following insights might help explain how deer and related big game take advantage of a distinct visual advantage over predators, including humans:

1) The pupil of hoofed animals dilates wider to emit more light (and the light-gathering property of the eye increases with the square of the pupil's diameter); 2) A deer's retina is packed with specialized "rods," sensitive to short-wavelength light, necessary for keen low-light vision; 3) Ungulates have a unique reflective layer of pigment—tapetum lucidum—that gives them a "second chance" to gather light once it passes through the retina; 4) The lens of an ungulate's eye lacks a filter to block ultraviolet light (humans are endowed with such a yellowish filter).

These deductions led to a new generation of UV-blocking products in the recent past. Whether inferences from pig research can be attributed to whitetail deer remains to be seen (no pun intended) but I am confident that no major camouflage manufacturer adds ultraviolet brighteners to its dyes; however, commercial non-scented detergents might pose a problem, making ATSKO's U-V Killer a viable option. Otherwise, wash hunting duds with unscented sport soap (preferably with Triclosan to control BO-generating bacteria) and stop worrying about "glowing in the dark."

The net result is that ungulates "see hundreds of times better in dim light than humans," Dr. Neitz says. Other researchers I've queried on the subject, including Dr. James Kroll, agree that deer have amazing vision. Consider the common sight of a buck bounding effortlessly through dense underbrush during a New Moon period so dark you couldn't see your hand in front of your face without a flashlight. Perhaps this is why deer seem crepuscular (active during low-light periods) at some times and nocturnal (no-light periods) at others. (The ever-adaptive whitetail shifts feeding schedules with the weather. During warm months of the year, deer are most often observed at dawn and dusk when it's coolest; in the winter and during periods of unseasonably cold temperatures deer are often on the move in midafternoon to late-afternoon.)

Now for the flip-side to the vision coin: Humans endowed with an abundance of color-sensitive, long-wavelength "cones" see better than ungulates in bright light. Consequently, deer and their hoofed brethren lay low during the brightest part of the day to reduce exposure to predators, who may exploit a visual advantage. This doesn't necessarily mean deer will interrupt twice-daily feeding forays, though. Their chambered stomachs crave a rhythmic cycle and still growl in harmony with

During this lunar period, bucks feed within heavy cover; relocate and score.

70

Moon times. Deer continue to nibble cautiously on acorns, forbs, greenbrier, aspen leaves and shoots—any food source sprouting within cover.

You can use these insights to kill a buck, but it won't be easy. When confronted with middle-of-the-day Moon times associated with new and Full Moons, you must desert open food sources and the transition zone. To wit: relocate closer to bedding areas. And those who won't or can't hunt all day, must set their hunting watches to an unconventional shift.

"This is a 'can't win if you don't enter' sweepstakes," Myles says. "Gotta hunt hard all day. Slacking off for lunch or breaking for a noontime siesta is a big mistake."

Other factors work against hunters at this time:

- The window of movement seems less concentrated. Like fish during a full and New Moon, a few deer may feed at 11 a.m., some not until 2:15 p.m. You never know. This makes all-day vigils for stand-hunters, as Myles alluded to above, standard policy.
- Deer travel is best measured in minutes, not hours, for two reasons. First, deer feed quickly at midday. Second, they don't snack much in the morning when moving from nighttime bedding areas to daytime bedding areas; they make a beeline to their destination, with little or no meandering.
- Whitetails are ultra-spooky when they lack the psychological comfort of low light.

"Deer either don't move much during the day, or they stick to the shadows of far-away cover when they do," Bob Zaiglin says. "It's a humbling time for most hunters." Registration statistics bear this out. I recently checked the numbers for St. Louis County in my home state of Minnesota and found that fewer deer were registered during a Full Moon than at any other lunar period. No wonder some Delaware hunters lobbied to switch the deer opener away from Full Moons (this fueled a study that failed to document poor hunting during this lunar period, but an influx of hunters in the woods on opening day likely influenced the results).

Add it up, and it doesn't add up: Less exposure means reduced odds for hunters, especially those sticking to typical morning/ evening shifts. A graphic illustration of what I'm talking about was borne out by my friend Steve Shoop, who runs a top-notch bow camp in northern Missouri. In the pre-dawn darkness during a Full Moon period, Shoop dropped a hunter off at a stand that was surrounded by scrub oaks on a sidehill—an excellent area to hunt midday bedded bucks. Indeed, when it was light enough to see, the client noticed a big buck bedded no more than 75 yards away. But all the hapless bowhunter could do was glass the deer from a distance. "The poor guy sat on the edge of his seat all day without ever drawing his bow," Shoop said. "He couldn't get down and stalk the deer because it was facing him. And the buck never moved from its bed—not even

Midday is no time to slack off during a New or Full Moon.

once to get up to take a leak."

This episode took place during the post-rut, when experienced bucks refrain from hounding does, instead resting up for the next real breeding session. Perhaps you agree that hunting tactics must be retooled. Let's locate some beds and engineer some hunts geared specifically for this most difficult lunar period.

Uncovering The Beds

General bedding areas are relatively easy to predict. Specific spots, however, are difficult to pinpoint, let alone hunt. Bucks are extremely wary and secretive about where they hole up for the day, and the areas where they do are almost impossible to enter without being winded, sighted or heard. If you've done your homework, you've probably uncovered most of the daytime beds deep in thickets along the edges of hilltops or knolls (urine deposits in the snow and the presence of early rubs are dead giveaways). Such strategic positions allow bucks to taste rising thermals while constantly testing prevailing winds behind them and swirling eddies to the front and sides. Thus, the rise in elevation offers a three-fold advantage: improved visibility, enhanced hearing and ideal scenting conditions, thanks to current shifts and backdrafts.

A notable exception involves certain topographical barriers. As mentioned previously, a buck can easily hear or see danger coming from a nearby swamp (while testing winds at his backside). So any bog, pond, lake or river with good strip cover tips the odds in favor of the buck. He knows where predators are likely to come from and has reserved a handful of escape routes for a quick exit. Still, if the terrain rises a mere five or 10 feet, the buck will likely use it.

Draw Upon The Wind

During blustery conditions, deer pull a Houdini by retiring in draws, coulees and the lee sides of drainages. During a recent Kansas bowhunt, I watched a 150-class buck spring from his bed in a small patch of prairie grass at the intersection of two dry creeks. If a yearling buck that was chasing a reluctant doe hadn't tripped over the bedded monarch, I wouldn't have given the area a second thought. Mule deer enthusiasts who know the spot-and-stalk gambit well are a step ahead of this game. With a little experience, you begin to get a sixth sense for the cubbyholes bucks tend to choose.

Outfitter Steve Shirley says he invariably sees his biggest Kansas bucks while guiding quail and prairie-chicken hunters. "The dog goes berserk and I can feel it coming," he says. "A little patch of buck brush at the head or tail of a draw tucked away in the middle of nowhere is a big-buck magnet when the wind howls."

Incidentally, I hunted with Shirley, who heads up Walnut Valley Guide Service, headquartered out of Arkansas City, Kansas, and accurately predicted how the week-long hunt would pan out. When I asked Shirley if late mornings had produced more buck sightings than the first hour of daylight, he gave me a double-take. "We *have* been seeing a lot of bucks around 10:30," he said. Later, after sizing up two parcels of land Shirley gave me free reign to hunt, I sensed things would go slow until the end of the week—when the Moon favored a late-afternoon hunt. Which is exactly what happened: Shirley arrowed a tall-tined Pope and Young buck within 15 minutes of a sunset Moon time. "You made a believer out of me!" he said with a wide grin when I pulled into his driveway. "Your

Take your time glassing draws when the wind howls. Especially check out scattered clumps of buck brush!

Moon stuff is uncanny."

A final key for zeroing in on beds is distinguishing daytime bedding areas from nighttime bedding areas. Recall that deer prefer bedding at lower elevations and in open terrain in the evening—where cool air settles and deer can see greater distances in the reduced light. Be sure not to confuse beds and related sign along field edges, glades and forest openings. These are nighttime-only spots! As usual, there's an exception out there in the swamps, which I'll get into in a bit.

That Fool Moon

Hunting's usually best around sunrise and sunset when the Moon peaks over-head (or underfoot), mainly because the lunar pull on big game coincides with low light. The Full Moon period is another scenario, one with a cosmic twist. Most hunters believe deer are active throughout the night "in the bright light of the Moon" and therefore are inactive during daylight hours. This is actually a half-truth. Tom Indrebo, producer of the acclaimed video, "Monarch Valley," saw a different picture unfold while logging 5,000 hours spotlighting and filming deer after dark over a 10-year period. Indrebo couldn't escape the rule of the Full Moon night:

"I learned not to do much spotlighting [then]," he told me. "Most deer don't show themselves till midnight or so, and that's too late for me to get anything [on tape] and get back at a reasonable hour."

But, like so many aspects of deer behavior, there's an exception to this rule, one that hunters would do well to take advantage of:

"Give me a rising Full Moon and a setting sun in January," says Bo Pitman,

73

Why does Bo Pitman like a rising Full Moon and setting sun in Alabama during January?

head guide at White Oak Plantation near Tuskegee, Alabama, "and I'll be in whitetail heaven." Pitman's commercial operation, located in the deer-rich black-belt soils of central Alabama, affords the guide the luxury of testing theories and strategies on a remarkably stable population of mature bucks. The key to this bewitching time window, he says, is the extra half-hour of twilight a rising Full Moon gives hunters (where legal hunting hours extend past sunset). The extra dose of moonlight becomes a buck's worst nightmare when he assumes light is fading and it's actually intensifying.

If you look in the right places, the documentation there. As an example, last December, four deer were hit by cars during a single rising Full Moon in Hermantown, a suburb of my hometown of Duluth, Minnesota. All the accidents took place within 10 minutes. I'm sure hectic road traffic at the end of the work day contributed. But it's fact, not folklore, that deer often move in short bursts in late fall when the Moon rises as the sun sets.

This trait appears to be a seasonal, however. In the summer, for instance, few deer feed in open fields at dusk during Full Moons. Conversely, the New Moon period seems to trigger minor end-of-day activity, starting with does, ending up with bucks. But day in and day out, most deer are active at sunrise and sunset when the Moon peaks overhead and underfoot. The reason few hunters' field notes reflect this is because they "remember" Full and New Moon periods better than Moon positions expressed as Moon times.

In sum, three distinct tactics unfold when the Moon exerts maximum influence from midday overhead or underfoot positions. Hunt midday:

1) close to food sources or transition zones, if deer bed a considerable distance away (there must be adequate cover along the way);

2) near food sources associated with heavy cover, when deer bed fairly close

to open food sources (key on acorns in the Midwest and South and thickets like prickly pear in Texas);

3) within security cover and forget food sources.

A fourth option is one that few hunters know about—catching a buck switching midday bedding areas. Be forewarned that time and patience are prerequisites. No matter how hard or smart you hunt, if you spook the buck, you'll end up losing the cat 'n' mouse game. As Zaiglin says, "Deer are incredibly adaptive to their surroundings, almost invincible to human resources ..." That's why we need another Myles Keller trick to tackle this ticklish situation.

Close But Not Too Close

Myles hunts buck bedding areas… when he has to. They aren't his first choice, because they're a touchy place to hunt.

"The actual bedding area is usually my last-resort effort. I hate to sound like a broken record, but my entire game plan revolves around not pressuring a buck; if he's at all nervous, he'll tiptoe clear around me to make the most of his nose. So I stay out of an area—or I stay on stand all day—in hopes the buck will stick to his routine and maybe get a little lazy. Then I can usually score.

"But if I have to go for it, I've got to know a spot well enough to hunt it properly. I've been on many out-of-state hunts and thought I was on the right track, only to find I had to spend more time gathering information to get in the ball game. I like to look for a unique combination—cover with good density that's difficult to approach yet has relatively easy access to feed. And, of course, there can be no local pressure from two-legged predators—those bucks fearing for their lives will dive into No Man's Land.

"In most cases you have to hunt a bedding area sparingly. The lone exception is a woodlot along a river bottom. Here you can approach [the beds] from several different angles, even from the water in the dark. Still, no matter how careful you are, you'll lose more times than you'll win hunting near deer beds. For instance, the game is over if the buck's already bedded when you sneak in under a flashlight. I

Myles has become a Riverbottom Master, and for good reason—these areas are made for bowhunting because bucks must compromise wind direction along river bends. Still, he had to wait this buck out.

75

just cringe when I hear a single deer bounding off in the brush ahead of me; I pretty much know it's a buck, and I'm back to Square One.

"The mating season has a big impact on this tactic. I have to do more experimenting, but I'll be looking closely at the Moon when I check for doe bedding areas as the rut unfolds. That's when breeding bucks set up 'temporary beds' just downwind from [bedded] does. Know where the ladies lie down to chew their cud, and hang a stand close but not too close. You see evidence of bucks relocating like this time and time again: Gun hunters drive a woodlot that no one ever suspected held a good buck. Then, bingo! a monster buck boils out of the woodwork. What really happened is that this animal had been bedding safely most of his life in a secluded spot, but just happened to get caught by the drivers in that silly woodlot (I say silly because it's such an obvious spot to drive). Anyway, the buck was out of his element checking for does coming into heat. He got caught. So I frequently hunt downwind of these 'temporary beds' during the rut, particularly when the in-between zone doesn't seem to be clicking.

"I keep tabs on the buck's main security beds, too. During midday, a buck may go to water or relocate from his temporary bed to his 'secure bed' until nightfall. Or, he may move from security cover to a vantage point where he can again prospect for hot does. When I look at a spot, years of hunting run through my mind as I try to plug past experiences into the big picture. I'll never forget that Iowa buck that set up in the CRP. Took me two weeks to figure him out."

Lessons From Iowa

Myles' account of his Iowa monster, netting $162 \frac{2}{8}$ points, tagged on December 1, 1991, beautifully illustrates the security/temporary bedding phenomenon.

"This was a frustrating hunt even though I knew one thing right away: By the fresh tracks in the picked cornfield, it was obvious the deer were limited to one major food source, and they were really working it over. That helped narrow the options down, or so I thought. I also had the big buck's general bedding area pegged by his rubs in two sections of woods, one of which I tried to hunt, but couldn't simultaneously monitor a CRP field and a harvested beanfield from my stand. At least by eliminating this area I knew when it was time to commit myself a little closer and a little deeper. So I hung a stand on the CRP side to be able to survey the woods and the picked cornfield at the same time. I still wondered exactly where that buck was bedding... I never saw him in the field during legal hunting hours and couldn't catch him coming back in the morning.

"Anyway, from my new vantage point I noticed a heavy trail cutting through the CRP field with my binocs. Were some deer bedding in the tall grass? Was the buck down in the corner, just off the doe beds? The addition of CRP cover is great for pheasants, but it adds a new dimension to bowhunting whitetails! I eventually discovered what this buck was up to. Sometime during the day he'd leave his security bed, down at the corner of a wooded thicket, and bed in the CRP. This move let him sniff out each and every doe as she entered the field at day's end. Then, after all the deer had passed and darkness fell, the buck would join the party in the field.

"Now, I didn't know this when I set up a third stand slightly deeper, still overlooking the CRP. But I figured I'd get a good shot if the buck slipped up and headed for the field before dark. Well, my move paid off, though not exactly as

I'd planned. From my last observation stand I saw this horse of a buck methodically bobbing his massive head above the broom grass. The trail jogged to within 30 yards, and I was at full-draw by the time the buck hit the corner. It was high noon when my arrow found its mark. I still don't know why bucks switch beds during the day like this, but this fella sure had a cozy setup: Deer coming out from behind as well as in front; tall grass all around; other deer acting as sentries when they preceded him into the field;

The story behind this 160-class Iowa buck teaches an invaluable lesson about hunting security and temporary beds during midday.

scent-checking does for a receptive breeding partner without exposing himself.

"Every buck doesn't pull this, but it happens often enough to keep on the lookout during midday. If a guy can set up close, but not too close, he's got a fighting chance."

A final footnote rounds out the story. I've noted the difficulty of hunting this lunar period, which essentially boils down to the double whammy of reduced deer activity in tough-to-hunt areas. I personally believe this Iowa buck was responding to the Moon's increased electromagnetic forces. He didn't need to move. The wind hadn't shifted. And he wasn't pressured from any hunter, dog or coyote. I think the buck just got a little antsy. After all, he could have slipped into a staging area as the sun set and waited for total darkness. But no, he made his move right at midday, a period most hunters consider a waste of time.

> Hunting his buck with conventional wisdom,
> Earl took off early, but still missed him.
> If he'd heeded the Moon,
> He would have hunted at noon,
> But Earl just couldn't buck the system.

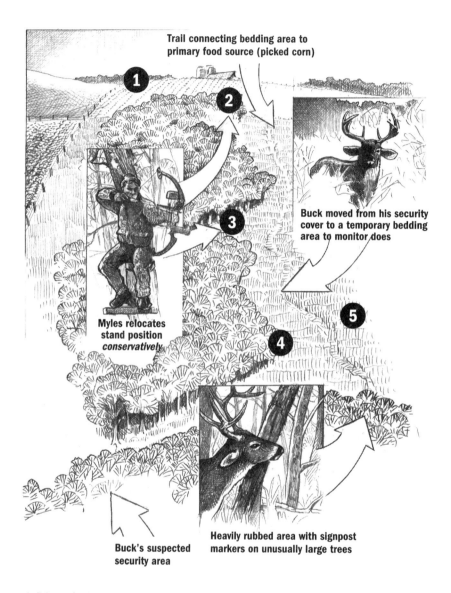

Trail connecting bedding area to primary food source (picked corn)

Buck moved from his security cover to a temporary bedding area to monitor does

Myles relocates stand position *conservatively*

Buck's suspected security area

Heavily rubbed area with signpost markers on unusually large trees

1. Primary food source: picked corn
2. First treestand relocation
3. Second treestand relocation and point of kill
4. Third (unused) treestand
5. CRP (Conservation Reserve Program) plot

Cornstalkin'

All of the strategies discussed so far rely on some deer movement, which makes hunting from a fixed position a deadly technique, especially for bowhunters. (Pope and Young statistics reveal that during a typical two-year scoring period, 80 to 85 percent of all entries are arrowed from a treestand.) But what if bucks don't or won't budge? Remember Steve Shoop's story about that Missouri buck that racked up from dawn to dusk in one spot? Obviously, a bedded buck, compared to one that's up and moving, is not a good candidate for traditional ambush tactics. Even rattling and calling don't seem to fare well when bucks are on their bellies (just ask Larry Weishuhn). Your frontline mission, then, should always be concentrating on peak Moon times so as to hunt deer on the move. Nevertheless, sometimes you've got to go to them to make something happen.

Take standing corn. A wet fall used to ruin a lot of Midwest bowhunts before enterprising archers learned the secret of cornstalking. Because of the constant rustling of brittle stalks, sneaking up on wary whitetails isn't as difficult as it sounds. Deer expect to hear noise, and they often hesitate when you draw within range. Furthermore, the same cover that conceals deer also camouflages a hunter on foot.

And speaking of camo, of all the designs I've tested over the years, Backland is without peer in corn country. A hunter just melts like butter into the scene with this pattern. It's also effective in open prairie.

As one might expect, some cornfields offer better hunting than others. A Wisconsin study involving six small cornfields, ranging from one to five acres, disclosed that:

- Deer preferred fields adjacent to wooded tracts.
- Some deer traveled up to 900 yards to feed in the corn.
- The largest field received the lightest traffic.
- The later into the season corn remained standing, the more deer used it to the exclusion of other feed.
- Deer fed more on corn spilled onto the ground than corn still in the ear.
- Hungry deer typically targeted corn rows along the edges more than interior rows.

Keep in mind that this study

I'm sizing up a Missouri cornfield that looks ripe for a cornstalk. If not, I'll get Steve and Jill Shoop to help me sweep it clean of bucks.

involved mainly feeding deer. But whitetails often use corn as cover, and larger fields are chosen because vastness adds security. Of special import are "missed" cornrows that somehow did not take or were not planted. Weedy strip-cover gives deer excellent protection, and these areas should be carefully noted (keep in mind that in some parts of the corn belt crops are rotated).

Regarding the actual stalk, it's no big mystery. Simply pick a favorable configuration with a good headwind or crosswind and sneak *across* the rows. As you get to each open row, peek s-l-o-w-l-y up and down before slipping through the stalks and into the next row. Once you've made it to the outer row, turn up the field, moving into the wind, and sneak ahead a short distance (about as far as you could see in the corn). Then swing back for another cross-corn session. You must be careful to err on the conservative side when deciding how far to move ahead, or you could step on a buck just out of sight.

Suppose the cornfield runs north/south and the wind's out of the northwest. You cut across the corn rows on the south end, heading east to west. Then you move north about 30 or 35 yards before re-entering the field and heading east against the grain. You move up a shorter distance than you could readily see just in case a buck was lying just beyond view.

That's about it... except when the wind blows against the corn rows rather than with them. Then you have to backtrack all the way around each time you hit the end row or you risk bumping deer.

As for bumping deer, nothing's worse than creeping within bow range of a good buck and inadvertently stumbling onto a bedded doe. You gingerly side-step the ladies! You might be able to skirt this problem by targeting likely buck-only spots such as depressions in the field, rock piles and other obstructions that remain hidden when the crop matures. (Hint: Glass these areas in the spring before the growing season).

In late fall you can track a buck in corn by following its trail in the snow. Follow the tracks up the row until they disappear, then carefully poke your head into the row to your left or right to pick up the trail again.

Sweep 'Em Off Their Feet

Myles sometimes pushes deer in cornfields with a patented "sweep." "As far as I'm concerned, the 'tapered sweep' is the best way for bowhunters to nudge deer in a corn patch," he says. "No other method controls deer movements with the kind of precision bowhunters need to get a close shot." If you're game, here's the layout.

Start by spreading out your buddies so that the first guy's staggered ahead of the second, who's ahead of the third and so on; depending on the size of the field, you'll need anywhere from four to six bowhunters.

Always work into the wind with a blocker set up in the far corner. It's imperative that the deer have a headwind, but a slightly quartering wind also works. "No buck worth his headgear is going to bust out *with* the wind," Myles says. "Any game plan ignoring this principle usually ends up with deer doubling back and frustrating the entire hunt. Oftentimes guys don't even see any deer although they could've been as close as a cornrow or two away."

You might be wondering how a blocker positioned upwind can avoid spoiling the push. "If you do it right," Myles says, "the scent stream of the stander is surprisingly narrow." The accompanying illustration explains what Myles is talk-

"Blocker" in far corner of field

Bedded bucks will end up in the Northeast corner of this field

"Drivers"

Tapered "drivers" push cornfield against the rows

ing about. This ingenious plan produces as often as it fails for four solid reasons. First, the deer are pretty much hemmed in because they don't have many options; they want to stay in the cover so they reluctantly retreat for the far corner. Second, although the stander appears to be upwind of the deer, they can't possibly pick him up until it's too late. Third, a good buck is usually the last one out because he's learned to use other deer as sentries. When he meets the "end of the row," he'll likely focus on other deer boiling out in the open, and this should give the blocker plenty of time to get off a quality shot. And fourth, each hunter on foot has decent a chance to get a shot. (Incidentally, this setup works best if the cornfield is adjacent to open country; deer are hesitant to leave the security of the corn, and by the time they've reached the end of their rope, it's too late.)

Double Trouble At High Noon

Marty and Scott Glorvigan are twin brothers from Grand Rapids, Minnesota who've perfected a little push that's the slickest I've seen in the thick stuff. Two—and only two—bowhunters are necessary for pulling off the "double trouble" deer drive. "It's all based on common sense," Marty said. "If you have a good idea of where a buck is likely to go, extra hunters introduce unnecessary competition and confusion. Big drives with droves of hunters might be necessary in some patches of woods, but not where we go."

At first blush it's hard to imagine how a pair of bowhunters could possibly corner a buck in heavy timber. With his incredible nose and excellent eyesight and hearing, a jumped buck can be an elusive quarry for a dozen hunters toting guns. However, this unique drive is effective with only a pair of hunters because it controls key variables and takes advantage of a peculiar trait of whitetail deer.

"Some places are unhuntable with any method, if the buck can wind you from several directions." Marty says. Meaning, the Glorvigans avoid certain topographical features—gullies, ridge saddles, high ridgetops—that cause winds to swirl. And large, flat wooded areas are impossible for two men to cover. "That's why we concentrate on narrow strips of cover," Scott says. "If the deer don't have many options, we can usually intercept them."

So head for "corridor cover" that constricts deer movement. And the narrower the better. Fingers of high ground separated by swamps really pop out on a topo map. "Unless deer are extremely pressured," Marty says, "they tend to follow the path of least resistance, which is going to be the high ground."

Now these fingers aren't very impressive on a map or in person, especially compared to an oak ridge or a rolling stand of mixed popple and evergreens. But lowland fingers attract plenty of bucks and few hunters. So if at all possible, avoid accessible tracts and pack into the hinterland, and you can deal with deer that will react to your two-man push in a predictable manner (pressured bucks are not easy to push).

In this setup you need a point man (lead) and a swing man (trailer). The main duty of the point man is slowly flushing out corridors of travel (bucks don't stick to runways like does). Occasionally, the point man may catch the movement of a deer ahead and signal the trailing hunter into position with prearranged hand signals. The leader also reads sign along the way and is responsible for interpreting and responding to ever-changing conditions. For example, one time the duo had trailed a nice set of tracks in the snow for several hours when Scott noticed a second deer joining the trail. About a 100 yards later, the trails split. Scott realized he'd goofed when Marty saw a large doe pause in front of him... but no buck.

As for the swing man, he stays in view of his partner at all times—typically 50 yards back or so. When a second hunter dogs the first in this manner, rather than hunting directly abreast or straddling off to one side, two important stumbling blocks are hurdled. The first is safety. "I always know where my brother is," says Marty, "and he always knows where I am. Deer drives can be nerve-wracking but not this one; it's as safe as hunting solo."

The other potential problem is intercepting a double-backing buck. For a very good reason, whitetails in a survival mode like to circle their pursuer rather than bound ahead for parts unknown: Their noses have already sniffed out the immediate area, and staying put is safer than dashing headlong into unscented cover. So when they sense danger from their backtrack, they prefer pausing frequently to test the wind rather than bolting. The end result is deer performing a little button-hook—jumping ahead behind some cover, then curling predictably off to the side. And now you know why the swing man must trail directly behind the leader: If the first hunter bumps a deer without getting off a shot, the second should be in perfect position for a clean kill.

"The shot's usually standing-broadside," Marty says. "I mean, deer are so preoccupied with Scott that they don't have a clue to my whereabouts. I've taken a lot of bucks that stood and watched Scott pussyfoot by." The mental picture you're likely to see when you release your arrow is your partner in one corner of your eye, and the buck standing still as a 3-D target, staring confidently over his shoulder.

Not all pushes end up with a tagged buck. If you get close but don't get to smoke the stogie, here's something you can do to boost your odds next time out:

Note exactly how the deer reacted and make necessary adjustments now. If you need to prune a little sight lane at a particular bottleneck, do it. Also, map out the routes deer took. I'll bet the next time you pull a little push, the deer will repeat their previous pattern.

Finally, keep in mind that you and your partner are sneaking along like a pair of ermines so that squirrels don't scold and crows don't caw. When you do this properly, you should get the same results as treestand hunting: close shots at standing deer. So the next time deer aren't on the move, push yourself to pull a little deer drive.

Secrets Of The Bog Bucks

It's no secret that swamps affect deer hunting, especially when hunter pressure mounts. Whitetails don't mind getting bogged down in the mire, where face-slapping cover and boot-sucking muck give them the upper hand. 'Tis no place for the average two-legged predator. You need a lot of luck and some kind of edge to beat the bog. Though I can't do anything about luck, I believe I've discovered the key for unlocking the swamp buck mystery.

About 20 years ago, I helped an old-timer drag a big buck out of the woods. "Listen," he whispered, his eyes darting nervously like windshield wipers. "If you can keep a secret I'll show you where I got this bugger."

I didn't know if the guy was putting me on or if he was just lucky, but I had nothing to lose. After we hoisted his buck onto the bed of his Chevy pickup, we backtracked through a hardwood ridge and clawed our way through a snarled alder brush pocket. About 15 minutes later the terrain lifted. Popples and birch and balsams dotted the landscape.

"Well, this is it," the old-timer announced, hands on hips. As he blew his sausage-like purple nose into a red-and-black paisley hanky, I realized that "it" was *it*. The two-acre patch of high ground was surrounded by swamp-loving tag alders. Talk about a whitetail moat and castle! After circling the island, I counted more

83

buck sign than I'd seen in a week. I mean, the place was laced with rubs and beds and droppings. And it reeked with buck musk, too. The old-timer wasn't lucky. He knew what "it" was all about.

To a buck, a "swamp island" is like a quaint bed 'n' breakfast. All of his daily needs—food, comfort, safety—lavishly surround his daytime lair. That is, until the mating urge hits and the drawbridge to his castle in the quagmire rises.

Two-thirds of the battle is finding huntable swamp islands, which are quite common throughout much of the nation. As usual, start with some serious paperwork to avoid busting through bogs only to find nothing worth hunting. The time-honored topographical map is a tremendous shortcut, if you know how to read swamp islands (not just any swamp island will be a deer magnet during the hunting season).

First look for the funky marsh symbol on the map, and get a feel for how swamps are laid out in relation to knolls, ridges and roads. Next, zero in on those features with the highest potential—patches of high ground ranging from two to 10 acres, ideally not too far from primary food sources (larger islands aren't nearly as huntable, and those too far back don't lodge many bucks).

On a contour map, the islands show up as minor changes in elevation *within* the marsh symbol. A simple circle, or doughnut-like double-ring in the marsh is a dead giveaway of higher ground surrounded by the wet stuff. Use aerial photos to reveal the kind of vegetation you're likely to encounter in a particular wetland. Dark shades indicate spruce bogs, medium-gray could be cedar, and lighter tones are probably open marsh or alders. Cross-check your findings with the topo map, which shows unforested areas as white, and don't forget the trick of enlarging and overlaying the two maps.

How do you hunt the mire? Once again, understanding the lunar cycle makes this game more hit and less miss. Let me count the ways:

- First and foremost, make sure the island is home to a good buck. Either glass deer heading in or out, or visit the island and look for rubs. If numerous trees aren't freshly polished, keep looking. No rubs, no bucks.
- It's critical that you beat the buck to his hideout (bump him just once in his

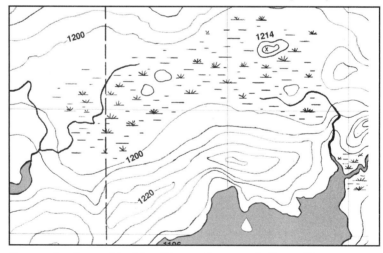

There are four "swamp islands" on this map. Can you make them out?

84

little moated castle, and you can forget about seeing him again). This usually rules out small bogs during midday Moon times because you can't maneuver close enough without getting picked up.

- An early morning Moon time is a better bet. Get nestled in and intercept the late-arriving buck who either nibbles his way in or dogs does into the morning hours. Better be there early, though. (A handy accessory for hands-free navigating in the dark is a Nite Ize adjustable head band that accommodates mini-flashlights. RCP Enterprises, Inc., 2525 Arapahoe Avenue, Suite E4-277, Boulder, CO 80302; 800-678-6483.)

- For a late-afternoon Moon time, pick a narrow swamp island pointing to a finger of oaks (preferably ripe with acorns). Set up where the finger and swamp meet, and waylay the buck coming out to snack or look for girlfriends.

The key to swamp islands is pressure. Bucks avoid hunters by bedding in out-of-the-way clumps of willows, tag alders, cedars, black spruce cattails—you name it.

So get out there. Just do it.

How To Reed A Buck

Sometimes you have to hunt the swamp itself. In transition, prairie and agricultural habitat, whitetails often dive into the eye-high cover of sedges, reeds and cattails. These hide 'n' seek whitetails can be had by deer hunters masquerading as duck hunters—get out the hipboots and wade in there!

I say this after making the mistake of avoiding a certain cattail swamp along the Platte River bottom in Nebraska, which cost me a 160-class whitetail. After a 10-year closure, a waterfowl refuge had been opened to bowhunting to control exploding deer numbers, and my friend Gayle Verbeck invited me down for the opener. A couple of years earlier, I'd arrowed a nice 150-class 8-pointer (pictured on page 56) while hunting with Verbeck, and I knew another great hunt awaited us.

It would have, had I taken the Moon into account. My second mistake was timing my arrival to coincide with a waxing Full Moon. Although Verbeck had glassed four Pope and Young bucks feeding toward the end of day in a food plot along the river bottom, we saw progressively fewer deer as we scouted before the season opened. Why did I discount the Moon on this trip? Because I figured a midday Moon was better than dealing with deer that had been pressured for a week. I mean, these adult deer had never heard the *ta-wang!* of a bowstring in their entire lives.

Well, I learned my lesson. As the Moon rose later each day in the Nebraska sky, deer made it to the food plots later each evening. Unfortunately, the configuration of the bottomland cover worked against my strategy. Picture standing corn and milo kissing open alfalfa; next to this were cattails as far as the eye could see. In other words, there were no corridors of cover, no funnels. Successful morning hunting hinged on deer lingering in the food plots before disappearing in the cattails after sunup; afternoon hunts required deer to make it to field edges before dark. It might have worked a week earlier, but now the Moon saw to it that deer remained in their beds until after dark. If only I'd relocated inside the cattails like a Denver, Colorado bowhunter who was rewarded with a 5 x 7 buck grossing in the 160s! Next time…

I heard this buck sloshing in the bulrushes for 10 minutes before he finally popped into view within arm's length of my camera lens.

The next time I get a chance to redeem myself, I'm going to follow the lead of Jim Hill, a Minnesota bowhunter who has made a science out of hunting bulrushes and cattail sloughs. Here's how to "reed" whitetails:

"First off, you've got to let the deer maintain a normal routine by keeping an effectively low profile," the sneaky Hill says. "Without the element of surprise, you don't have a prayer in a slough, because you'll be hunting in some very tight quarters." Bucks in reed habitat seem to have a sixth and seventh sense for detecting danger from afar. That's why Hill sneaks around "like a doggone coyote," frequently belly-crawling from patch to patch. One time he quietly chopped a hole in an iced-over slough so he could sit in just the right place to intercept deer. Another time Hill floated a piece of down to test wind currents, and watched the dancing feather settle on the moist nose of a quizzical doe.

"Once I spotted a buck trotting along a treeline," he said, "and all of a sudden the heavy-beamed eight-pointer slammed on the brakes. Would you believe that buck just stood in place, barely moving a muscle, for three hours straight?"

The reeds are troublesome to hunt, because you usually can't see deer coming until they're in your lap. You can't read body language nor can you use elevation to help control human scent.

Ingress and egress are critical, too. Hill suggests making your own network of trails and avoiding main deer trails. "[Your trails] will only be good for a short while, because pretty soon the deer will start using them," he says. "That's why you need enough spots to spread yourself around. Otherwise, deer could end up surprising you from downwind as you enter the slough."

Getting the shot opportunity is simple enough, and you can double or triple your odds by locating at the intersection of several trails rather than along trails leading in or out. Before you enter in, however, study the terrain for hidden topographical "channels" or "humps" within the reeds. Glass and glass and glass. The slough may look like a homogenous mass but you can read the reeds like a golf pro reads the manicured greens during the Masters at Augusta.

Getting the shot off takes planning. "You've got to be able to draw on an animal and not get picked up till your arrow is in flight," Hill says. "It gets downright hairy. If you cut back elaborate shooting lanes, forget it. Instead, a narrow sight window, with reed clumps in front to obstruct your drawing motion, is all you need. The lane into your 'blind' should form a little 'L.' Never let the sun backlight you either, because deer can easily pick up movement in diffused light."

Also, be real careful about calling deer. One time Hill grunted once too often, trying to turn a deer, and it backfired—the buck had him pegged "and that was that."

How far is the typical reed shot? Some bowhunters like to set back in the rushes a ways, shooting through a tunnel. Not Myles Keller. "I can reach out and practically touch a passing deer with the tip of my nocked arrow," he says. "I draw when I hear deer coming. With my Xi Extreme set at a reasonable hunting weight, I can take advantage of its improved 'effective let-off' and hold for quite a while if a group of does precedes a good buck."

Besides hipboots or waders, you'll especially appreciate a pair of accessories tailored for the mire. The first is a shoulder bow sling to hold your bow for extended periods. The best I've seen is the RediShot (32 Country Lane Court., St. Charles, MO 63304; 314-995-0912). The second is John Hambleton's Tote Stool (mentioned in Chapter 5). Because it clips to a belt and swivels on a dime, you can negotiate the mire with relative ease. You might need to improvise, though: To prevent the metal peg from disappearing in the ooze, cut a hole in the lid of a five-gallon bucket (spray paint it a dull color), and set the lid down first.

The Art Of Backtracking

While taking the escalator down to Concourse B at the Atlanta airport, I noticed that the steps descended about four inches faster than the railing; my hand, starting comfortably at my side, ended up scrunched behind my shoulder.

It took a while to pick up on it, and this is how it was when I discovered the true meaning of the art of backtracking.

I remember well the heavy snow piling up on the hood of my jacket like a snow cone. Whenever I'd bend down to duck under a balsam bough, snow would trickle down my neck and trigger a round of goose bumps. I'd had enough. As luck would have it, on the way out to my pickup, I bumped a buck. For some strange reason, I decided to follow its tracks backwards, toward a thicket I felt served as a primary bedding area—just to see what I could see.

Within a quarter-mile I hit several large beds. They were steaming fresh. But when I found a line of rubs, the last two piling up pungent bark shavings in the snow at the base of the

I intercepted this 270-pound buck after backtracking his Back 40 the previous fall.

tree, it suddenly hit me: The buck I'd jumped earlier was spending a lot of time back here during the day! Backtracking answers the questions traditional pre-season scouting only begins to raise. Which trails are used during the day? In the morning? Afternoon? Where are the bucks bedding with a northwest wind? A southeast wind?

Navigating in cyberspace on the Internet is fine for head knowledge. Here's field wisdom that will teach you the lifestyle of a buck in a matter of hours! Keep the following in mind when you decide to backtrack a buck to find out where he spends his time *during the day*:

• Be sure to cut a track made in the afternoon, not morning; you want to know where the buck hangs out during daylight, and afternoon trails are the only way to do it.

• Finding out where a buck has been today is no guarantee he'll be there again tomorrow… unless a strong influence encourages him to continue his ways. That force could be a primary scrape. Indeed, one of the best places to hunt in the deep woods where the deer herd is evenly balanced, is a deep, wide scrape. Big-woods bucks use these calling cards to their advantage in heavy timber, and backtracking a trail or three to a bedding area could be the ticket for hanging a stand in a strategic funnel.

- The best time to backtrack a buck is when you've glassed him from a distance and caught him relocating beds or monitoring his scrape line. Dash in and start snooping. Find out where he beds; where he's been feeding. Take notes on the wind and temperature, and don't forget the Moon times!

- Another excellent time to backtrack is right after the deer season. You may not be able to apply the information until the following year, but you'll get a good indication of the buck's normal routine. Chances are, he'll repeat it (jot down those Moon times, too). ○

Chapter 8

DOES THE MOON TRIGGER THE RUT?

Now that you've digested the preceding seven chapters, it's time for dessert. If questions seem to be falling like raindrops into a sea of shallow answers, it's because the rut needs to be wired into Moon strategies. First I'll sort out the rut phases so you won't be fazed by the ever-changing whitetail behavior in the fall. Next—are you ready for this?—I'll explain how a Michigan bowhunter uses the New Moon to plan the best hunting trip of his life. Last, I'll examine a technique ripe for trophy rutting whitetails during a key lunar period.

Gary Smalley, best-selling author and family counselor, articulates the main distinction between the sexes: Males are essentially in a constant state of sexual readiness, whereas females generally need something to get them ready. "Men have a sexual thought, on average, about every 20 seconds," he quips. If this is the case with humans, what about deer? During the rut, novice and veteran hunters alike can't help notice some bucks behaving like teenaged boys. Though much has been written about the advantages of hunting during the breeding season, most deer hunters I come in contact with still don't seem to get it...

The Rut Phase Craze

Contrary to popular belief, there are two distinct ruts in the whitetail world. The first ensures the propagation of the species; the second all but guarantees that deer hunters will return home scratching their heads instead of showing off some trophy headgear.

The first rut, of course, is the annual breeding season of deer. The second involves the many ill-conceived, fatally flawed strategies hunters have concocted over the years to take advantage of the only significant weakness of a slippery whitetail buck—his mating urge. I say hunters are stuck in a rut because they commit the same basic miscues at key times when deer behavior is actually quite predictable.

The key to bagging a whitetail will never change: Be in the right place at the

91

right time. As I've said many times throughout this book, we need to know what deer are doing now, not last month, last week or even yesterday. So here's a phase-by-phase blow on each stage of the rut. Time references reflect Midwest latitudes, where the rutting season commences earlier than in Southern states (e.g. peak rut is generally mid-November in the Midwest; December or January in the South and Southeast).

Phase 1: Sparring

Technically speaking, the rut begins when does go into heat. Then and only then will the ladies "stand" to be bred by a buck. Obviously, bucks interested in mating are vulnerable to lucky hunters—research shows that does become hyperactive within their core areas, and breeding bucks frequently venture far and wide of theirs—but this isn't the only time deer make mistakes. The early phase has its share of opportunities, even though it hasn't gotten the ink it deserves.

Around mid-September, so-called bachelor groups of two or more bucks are often seen feeding or bedding in close proximity to one another. A common misconception is that bucks are capable of breeding well before does enter estrus, so standard rut tactics (sex lures, mock scrapes, aggressive grunt calls and so on) should work. To the contrary, bucks are more interested in other bucks than does at this time. A hunter invading a buck fraternity expecting to arouse a sexual response is wasting his time. There are better options.

This initial phase is a special time of the year when the dominance hierarchy of bucks is sorted out by sparring: A pair of bucks square off in a pushing contest, with the stronger individual usually establishing his dominance. It's quite simple. Yet misunderstandings abound.

For one, don't confuse sparring with the ballyhooed technique of rattling. The

During the sparring phase of the rut, bucks are more concerned about their pecking order than does.

former is more like a shoving match; the latter is intended to mimic a down-and-dirty fight (which won't occur until later on). And by the way, don't let convincing stories of raging bucks battling to the bitter end mislead you. (Such fights are actually quite rare.)

Also, don't underestimate the sparring season. Sparring is a formality that bucks engage in everywhere. Clear winners and losers emerge, and the pecking order becomes well established before does enter estrus. Bucks older than 3 1/2 years don't spar as much as younger bucks that are less sure of their position in the hierarchy; they may spar among themselves long after dominant breeding bucks have ceased (turning their attention to the does).

With this in mind, why not take advantage of the sparring ritual? Antler tickling—not rattling—has drawn in many a buck that would have otherwise passed by out of range. There's nothing

I watched this doe lead the trailing buck around for about an hour before he finally bedded down about 75 yards away.

mysterious or complicated about the technique. Simply tickle a pair of antlers together periodically, then wait for a response. Keep in mind that a buck isn't likely to approach without any reservations; he wants to size up the competition before rushing into a match, so you must be on red alert at all times. My friend Wyatt Bream, a construction worker transplanted from Texas to the Upper Midwest, relates an example of what can go wrong, if you don't keep a grip on yourself.

"In South Texas, hunters rattle a lot but it never seems to work up here," he told me. "Then I tried 'tickling.' The very first time I touched a pair of antlers together, two bucks appeared—one to my right, the other to my left. Before I could draw my bow, they were pushing and shoving like a couple of sixth-graders at a school playground." Bream became so engrossed in the mock battle that when the bucks suddenly separated without warning, he reacted in slow motion; the bucks trotted away gracefully as the five-thumbed bowhunter fumbled to draw.

Antler tickling can be effective, because it arouses the natural curiosity of whitetail bucks when they're most curious. Try it later on, however, and all you'll probably see are spikes and forkhorns—dominant bucks won't respond because they've already earned their right to a share of does.

Where to tickle? Briefly, bucks in the sparring phase of the rut stick pretty much to a well-defined home range centered around a specific food source. Bucks eat more at this time of year than any other, and this is the key to intercepting them. In agricultural lands, you can't beat bean fields. In the south, "greenfields" planted with clover or ryegrass are favored. Just remember the Moon: inch back toward cover as the Moon peaks during increasing periods of daylight.

Phase 2: The Pseudo-Stage

This phase isn't included in any wildlife journal. But it's out there. As bachelor groups begin to disperse, bucks filter into predictable staging areas: downwind from social doe groups. The bucks are simply waiting for the first does to cycle. After all, they don't want to miss any action. By spending most of their time downwind from traditional doe bedding areas, dominant bucks can keep subdominant bucks at bay, too.

We've already discussed the significance of early-season rubs. You can find them without even looking for them—if you know how to identify the does' daytime bedding areas. "They're strategically situated for all sectors of wind, and they have plenty of shade from the sun and shelter from adverse winds," Myles says. "When you find a main bedding area, you'll know it by all the sign. The beds will always seem fresh. If you're in doubt, walk downwind about 100 yards or so. You'll see the rubs."

This stage isn't real productive, so you're better off laying back, playing the waiting game. Remember Myles' buck pictured on page 75 for which he waited till everything was right? That's the essence of trophy hunting. Use the Moon and your knowledge of how the rut changes deer behavior, then move in for the kill.

Phase 3: The Courtship

The staging game usually lasts about a week and bleeds into subsequent breeding cycles. A gradual rise in male hormone production and a marked change in the scent of does triggers this next phase. The real fun starts when, all of a sudden, bucks begin hunting for and harassing does. The courtship phase is a good time to be in the woods if you're the kind of person who wins lotteries: A buck's pattern breaks down now, and he could end up most anywhere a hot doe takes him.

Deer courtship is a strange phenomenon that many hunters misinterpret. They see does being trailed by adolescent bucks, noses to the ground like bloodhounds, even though most does are at least several days away from estrus. Experienced breeding bucks know this, of course, and about all you'll see early in this phase are teenagers that don't quite know how to handle their hormones.

Standard rut tactics apply at this time such as discriminant use of estrous deer lures (for those who believe in such products), tending-grunt calls, primary-scrape and rub-line monitoring and so on. You know this. But do you know how to read does?

Bucks aren't interested in blind dates during the tending stage of the rut; rather, bucks lead does out of the mainstream of deer travel, forcing you to hunt in some oddball places.

If you know how to interpret a doe's body language, you could nail a good buck by hardly trying. In a word, a hot doe is nervous. She's not quite ready to accept the aggressive advances of an infatuated buck, so she tolerates him only at a distance—well behind her, not alongside her. Studies indicate trailing distances vary from 150 feet to a quarter-mile. If the buck gets too close, the doe scampers off nervously.

How does this affect practical hunting strategy? First and foremost, hunt where the majority of does are feeding and bedding—doe sign, not buck sign, is paramount now. Second, keep up with the does' reproduction cycle, and be ready when a buck comes a courtin'.

Suppose you notice a fidgety doe tiptoeing past your treestand. Her tail's cocked, and she's plumb antsy. If she prances by out of range, I say you've got a sure bet if you hurry… Get down from your treestand and get on her trail pronto! A buck could be close behind, nose to nose with the woods floor. He won't notice you hunched beside a tree or bush.

Besides reading each doe's body language, glass her tarsal gland (located on the inside joint of both hind legs). As she comes into season, this gland turns from tan-brown to matted black. If her tail stands erect, cocked to the side, she's available and definitely looking. Which leads to the next rutting phase.

Phase 4: Tending (Breeding)

Many are the colorful (usually embellished) stories of bucks and does pairing off during the peak of the rut. I'm afraid I do not share the euphoric outlook of most writers concerning this time of the deer season. This is when luck, not game plans drawn from studious research and copious field notes, plays the biggest role. Though I've experienced plenty of luck in the past, it's never been the right kind. But if you've got the confidence of a home-run hitter when he gets on a 3-0 count and his third-base coach flashes the green light, here's what you're probably doing:

• Monitoring does around the clock, setting up in pockets where bucks steer does away from the main deer traffic. This is hard to do, but I've forced myself on at least two occasions in which it paid off during a time when I would have drawn blanks. Regarding productive areas, I know where they're not.

"It isn't where just about every seasoned bowhunter hangs a treestand," says popular video producer and game call manufacturer Mark Drury. "I leave those mesmerizing rubs and scrapes alone--because so will the bucks--and try to figure out where a buck could take a hot date an not be pestered by rivals. This is one of the few instances in which deer seem to act almost human-like." So, forget about traditional prerut courtship areas; bucks are busy tending does and aren't interested in blind dates.

• Situating yourself *between* doe social groups. Each family seems to stake out a little core area that it frequents on a regular basis. Set up between several, and you could catch a two-timing buck.

• While monitoring does, you're watching for weather conditions that could dictate wholesale diet changes; where you'll find the kitchen, you'll find the ladies.

Phase 5: Post-Rut & Recovery

As a general rule, between 60 and 80 percent of the does are bred during the first major estrous cycle. A doe remains in heat for about 24 hours, and if she isn't bred during this period, she'll likely cycle again approximately 25 to 29 days later in most areas of the country. Experienced breeding bucks know all good things must come to an end, but it takes them a few days to figure it out. Even then, they're eager for one more fling... When the demand of anxious bucks begins to exceed the supply of willing does, a special time unfolds.

After this, bucks begin to conserve energy, moving mostly to stretch or water for the next three days to a week. The recovery phase also takes hunters awhile to figure out what's going on. It seems that one day deer are popping up across the countryside like targets on a shooting gallery, and the next day only a fawn or two turns up. During this phase, breeding bucks are more difficult to kill than at any other time; they've come to their senses and are back in their comfort and safety mode. It's back to the bedroom for savvy hunters—even during early and late Moon times.

Fortunately, recuperation is short-lived. When the buck's up and taking nourishment, you want to see the Man in the Moon peaking overhead or underfoot early and late in the day. Depending on the area of the country, this could be the first half of December or as late as mid-January. Once again, key on food sources close to a buck's bedroom where he can make efficient beelines to and from his sleeping quarters.

By the time the buck's strength returns, another round of does enters estrus, and the mating ritual repeats itself. If you adopt a game plan that corresponds to the buck's *current* phase of behavior, you won't be fazed by seemingly contradictory events.

Does The New Moon Set The Rut?

Too cold. Too hot. Not enough rain. Too wet. Not enough bucks. Too many antlerless permits. Must have been last week. Too bad I have to work next week.

If the rut is such a big deal, why all the excuses for not scoring during this can't-miss time? Trouble is, the rut's so dang fickle. One year it seems to peak early, the next year, it's two weeks late. Or it hits like lightning for a couple of days (when you are working) or barely trickles along with little or no fanfare; then, just when you concluded the rut is a memory, a buddy exclaims, "By George, you shoulda seen all the bucks!"

Wouldn't it be nice if hunters didn't need clairvoyant powers to know exactly when rut activity peaks? Then timing each rut phase—especially courtship flurries—would be a dream come true. All we'd have to do is plug in the deer's lunar cycle and we could plan rut-hunts months, even years, in advance.

Forget the power of the Dark Side. And forget about Star Wars' hooded Emperor, with his eerie opaque eyes and grotesque face declaring, "It is all happening as I have foreseen." Veteran Michigan bowhunter Bob Scriver says anyone can predict the rut—he claims to have done so eight years in a row—with a simple New Moon formula. With it, he can gauge the timing, intensity and duration of the rut as well as predict the kind of subsequent rut(s) hunters will likely face.

"I've been bowhunting for over 20 years, and ever since I can remember I've kept a log on the Moon and related rutting activity," he said. "I'm absolutely convinced that the New Moon is the key to the rut."

Before we get into the details, let's review a few basic facts about the whitetail reproductive cycle. First, does coming into estrus determine peak breeding activity. "But there's often a substantial difference between 'peak of the rut' and 'peak breeding,'" says Bob Zaiglin. "The first is when the average hunter thinks deer are hyperactive, and the second is when the majority of does are actually being bred. The 'peak of the rut' occurs when bucks aggressively search for does, typically just before most of them come into estrus or just after estrus has been terminated. 'Peak breeding,' on the other hand, may actually be a relatively benign period as far as hunting excitement goes. We examine embryos in the spring here in South Texas to back-date for dates of conception, and they don't always line up with when we've seen the most bucks the previous fall."

Second, photoperiodism—the diminishing ratio of daylight to darkness—triggers the onset of the reproductive cycle. Just like when a buck's headgear begins to form, when longer days signal its pituitary gland to release testosterone, a doe undergoes a similar transformation in the fall—as the days become shorter, her pineal gland releases melatonin, a substance influencing the release of sex hormones from the pituitary. The pineal gland acts as a translator of photoperiod clues, and this is where the New Moon comes in.

"I see a cycle that's tied to periods of light and dark that just happens to coincide with the lunar cycle," Scriver said. "Is it any coincidence that the female cycle and the lunar cycle are [approximately] 28 days?" As previously noted, the Moon's face-to-face cycle is 29.5 days and its siderial cycle is 27.3 days; thus the average is 28.4 days. Studies on does showed spans of 28 and 29 days between successive heats in New York; 21 to 27 days in Upper Michigan; and 25 to 30 days in Minnesota.

Still, the variability begs explanation, as do hunter reports on inconsistent "rut dates" from fall to fall. "The New Moon is the answer," Scriver says. "A doe's pineal gland doesn't just measure waning sunlight, but it responds to all light, including that of the Moon. So it shouldn't come as a surprise that when a New Moon arrives earlier than a traditional rutting date for a given [genetic and geographic] deer population, the peak rut is skewed ahead of schedule.

"The doe's pineal gland tells [its pituitary gland] that the light is less, so 'the day must be shorter.' Estrogen levels then increase, and she cycles in heat. Poultry farmers have artificially manipulated light levels to enhance egg production for years. So has the Michigan DNR for boosting pheasant production. It's no big deal."

The "optimum length of day" is always

The does trigger the rut, and the New Moon helps determine the timing.

A buck behind every tree? Maybe ... if the demand exceeds the supply.

the starting point for determining traditional rutting dates. For example, in higher latitudes the rut begins earlier—daylight is shorter—with local exceptions of heavy snowfall (fawns must be birthed during favorable spring conditions). Next, factor moonlight, which can make the day seem longer or shorter, depending on its timing in the fall. For example, a lunation with a New Moon arriving a week earlier than a traditional peak rut date balances off the minute traces of extra daylight. The net result is an early rut.

For those interested in predicting future rut hunts, here's Scriver's formula. If a New Moon:

• Is "on time," coinciding with optimum daylight for estrous release: The rut will be electrifying for a short spell. The length of day is ideal for peak rutting, and so is the dark of the Moon. The frenzy will soon subside as does become bred and come out of estrus.

• Hits late: Most hunters will complain of a sub-par rut; however, chase activity will occur a week later, after a lot of hunters have given up prematurely. In states like Michigan, Minnesota and Wisconsin, many bucks will be harvested during the firearms season, with not enough remaining to service late-estrous does. Fewer does bred in November leads to an accelerated rut in December.

• Arrives a week early: The rut should be "decent," according to Scriver, arriving earlier and maintaining a fairly even keel. But if it's two weeks early, like it was in 1994 (November 3), rutting activity hits a moderate level and spreads out, with not much intensity. "The days are shorter, but the nights are darker," Scriver says. "The net effect is no change translated through the pineal gland. By the traditional rut date of November 15, daylight will be short enough to trigger a trickling rut, which will be spread out."

Don't forget the weather, either. A prolonged spell of thunderstorms and dark, overcast skies during the fall suppresses general deer activity. "I believe deer become depressed much like humans," Scriver says. "But a day or two after the clouds lift, the bucks often go bonkers; they've been cooped up at a time when they're free spirits, and if a few does come into a short period of heat, look out. This 'false heat' will quickly reverse itself, however, so you really have to stay on top of it."

Now that I've got your attention, here are a few New Moons to back-date:

Year	October	November	December
1993	10-15	11-13	12-13
1994	10-5	11-3	12-2
1995	10-24	11-22	12-22
1996	10-12	11-11	12-10
1997	10-31	11-30	12-29
1998	10-20	11-19	12-18
1999	10-9	11-8	12-7

The Full Moon & The Rut

There are two kinds of rattlers in Texas—snakes and antler-bangers. If you don't want to be lopped into the former camp, better learn the real secret to rattling the most dominant breeding buck in an area. It boils down to waiting for a Full Moon to overlap the rut. Four factors give you the best odds of the year for bagging the buck of many lifetimes.

First off, the Moon is underfoot at midday, so does will be up and feeding, whether or not they're in estrus. Of course, bucks know this, and they'll be on the prowl.

Second, the bright intensity of the Full Moon guarantees increased midday activity. "From 20 years of studying deer at night during Full Moons," Bob Zaiglin says, "I've witnessed a repeating sequence: Deer bed and feed all night long. Up at midnight, down by 1 a.m. Back up again at 3 a.m., and so on…" Deer seem to be unusually uncomfortable, and I suspect it's because of their perceived vulnerability to predation in the extra-bright light of the Moon.

Third, a Full Moon overlapping the rutting cycle is double trouble for dominant breeding bucks. "During the rut, bucks push does out in pear flats [cactus], running them ragged," Zaiglin says. "By sunrise the does will be holed up, and around midday they want to get up and flex, go to feed. Meanwhile, bucks continue pestering them. The typical three-day period of an estrous doe is no time to slack off at midday. Over the years, I and many of my clients have taken some impressive trophies at this time."

Which leads to the most important reason trophy hunters concentrate on this lunar period: The demand for does far exceeds the supply. "This fall, go out on a Full Moon night, and count the bucks you see," Scriver says. "I bet there won't be many. But if there was a hot doe out there, don't you think the bucks would be after her? Heck, they'll chase a doe in the middle of the day, if she's hot. But the fact remains, not many does will be in heat during the Full Moon. Two weeks later, you'll see some bucks chasing some does for sure."

No wonder rattling is a waste of time during the peak breeding season—when the supply of hot does is at its peak. A week or two later tells a different story. "The bucks are ornery because they can't find any action," Scriver says. "They've been running all night, and no doe will stand for them. They're on edge. A slight provocation could trigger them. Rattling when a Full Moon overlaps the rut can be deadly, if you happen to hit it just right."

Rattle Their Cage

In sum, during the Full Moon only bucks at the top of the totem pole get to breed. If you bump into a hot doe at this time, you've got a serious chance at a Booner. There will only be a handful of does in heat—the majority cycled during the New Moon—so the nature of the game has changed. Before, the supply met the demand; now, the demand exceeds the supply. The average hunter should be successful the first time around; savvy hunters could score now when the big boys will have been primed for a week or two.

The tactic of rattling is neither a science, nor an art. It's strictly a matter of timing, as alluded to earlier. Ideally, you want to rattle in a buck when he's on his feet and not preoccupied with a steady date. Larry Weishuhn, a former Texas state biologist, wholeheartedly agrees. Though he has successfully spotted bedded bucks in the distance and gotten a response from a rattling sequence, he'd much rather hunt an animal that's on the move. "It seems that once a buck decides to hole up for the day, he gets into a twilight-zone-type of mentality. Doo-do-doo-do. He isn't going to get up unless something really sparks a fire under him. I'd much rather rattle a buck I know is actively seeking does. That's one reason why I've hunted by the Moon for so many years."

Rattling also works best with a balanced deer herd. The two extremes of Texas and Canada are ideal candidates. When does badly outnumber bucks, the competition is next to nil, and the bucks rarely square off.

When it comes to rattling in the big woods, you can dismiss the need for low-impact scouting. Quietly erect a portable treestand along a hot rub or scrape line, and wait for the Full Moon to peak underfoot (typically 1 to 3 p.m.). Then rattle a pair of antlers, fairly softly at first, gradually increasing in intensity. Bang them together for 15 to 45 seconds. If you don't strike a responsive chord, try again in about 15 minutes. Then relocate, if you haven't sighted a whitetail within an hour or so.

Two final thoughts. Technically speaking, bucks do not grunt when they fight (the tending grunt is associated with a buck courting a doe); however, an adjustable grunt call still does the job in spite of the apparent contradictory message. But keep it simple. I've heard some so-called deer callers hit more notes than Whitney Houston, and I wonder what the deer think.

Last, add a decoy to your rattling sequence. Delta markets a realistic portable buck decoy that can be packed down and easily transported. (Delta/B-K Industries, 117 E. Kenwood St., Reinbeck, IA 50699; 319-345-6476.)

It's A Shoo-in

Now there's a right and wrong way to rattle a buck in the North Country. Like many hunters, I've learned all of the wrong ways. I'm starting to learn the fine line separating good, better and best techniques.

A good technique, for example, is doing my homework ahead of time to locate key traditional rutting territories. This should put me in an excellent position to trigger a buck before or after the rut peaks. A better technique is adding the Moon's influence to ensure that the buck is on his feet and most likely to investigate (compared to a buck bedded deep in the thick stuff). The best technique, however, is injecting efficiency. As noted bowhunter Dwight Schuh aptly points out, big-woods deer are neither as predictable, nor as plentiful as their open-country counterparts.

"I add a key wrinkle to the basic system," Schuh said. "I go to the bucks, instead of assuming they'll always come to me." The success of Schuh's strategy pivots around mobility. When I bowhunted with Schuh in Illinois recently, I watched him leave camp with his daily needs on his back. He didn't return until well after dark. With the help of his famous Dwight Schuh backpack, marketed by Fieldline, he could stuff needed accessories—from a survival kit to raingear—into a pair of removable Polar fleece-covered packs. Just as important, he strapped a super-lightweight portable treestand to his lightweight nylon composite frame.

Dwight Schuh rattled in this nice tall-tined Montana buck from a treestand.

"If a bowhunter rattles from the ground, even with the help of a buddy cleverly disguised off to the side, he might get a lot of sightings," Schuh explained. "But if he isn't elevated from the ground, he won't get many shots. I'd rather get one shot from, say, one or two encounters, than never draw my bow while sighting a dozen bucks that end up circling and blowing me off."

It's hard to argue with Schuh's success: *Sports Afield's* celebrated bowhunting columnist rattled up a pair of handsome bucks last year without trying. O

Chapter 9

THE NEW RUT RULES

I n the good old days, my Grandpa used to lick his chops when a chilly northwest wind signaled the first hint of fall. He knew, both intuitively and from experience, that the whitetail rut is best time of year to kill a hat-racked buck, as he used to call it. That's still true, but in spite of the Information Age we live in, many hunters head for the same woods with the same tactics on the same dates year after year. Talk about a rut!

It's high time for a change. I've learned a great deal since my theories on the rut were published back in 1995 in my book, MOONSTRUCK! In fact, I believe it's now possible to predict not only the rut, but each phase of the rut. This, in turn, tells us what to do as well as what not to do as deer undergo key physiological and behavioral changes in the fall.

Chapter 8's cursory examination of rut phases establishes a solid foundation for an emerging rut strategy. Now it's time to take rut-hunting to its highest level. There are new rules to the game.

Predicting the Rut

I admit to being possessed when it comes to figuring out how to time the rut. But I've got cold logic backing up my obsessive compulsive nature. If I really know when the breeding season kicks off, I will also know where to hunt and how aggressively I dare hunt. That, my friends, is the Whole Nine Yards. Ever wonder why it's possible to spook deer with rattling one day, yet rattle in the buck of a life a week later? You're about to get the straight scoop. The starting point is realizing that each rut phase presents both barriers and openings; discern the difference and you're razor-close to being at the right place with the right stuff.

Is the rut really that predictable? Two distinct factors say it is. The first is decreasing daylight, known as photoperiodism, referred to in Chapter 8. Suffice to say, thanks to her pineal gland, a whitetail doe is capable of "monitoring" light intensity at remarkably low levels. When daylight reaches a PRESCRIBED MINIMUM THRESHOLD, she prepares to enter estrus. Following the Fall

Equinox in September, daylight contracts as darkness expands. This is why deer in North America always breed in the fall (and why deer in the Southern Hemisphere breed during our spring, which is their fall). But because daylight hours diminish more rapidly in northern latitudes, particularly above the 40th parallel, rutting activity is generally more concentrated the farther north one travels.

A graphic illustration of this principle is the sunrise/sunset tables for the cities of Minneapolis and Houston, located near the middle of the Central Time Zone. According to the U.S. Naval Observatory, during the week of October 24-30 for a typical year, sunrise times for Houston change from 7:29 a.m. to 7:33 a.m. whereas Minneapolis sunrises change from 7:40 a.m. to 7:48 a.m. The sunset times also change--five and nine minutes, respectively, for the two cities. While the net difference over one week's time may seem insignificant--Houston loses about nine minutes of daylight, Minneapolis loses 17 minutes--the RATE of change for Minneapolis is nearly 100 percent greater.

Obviously hunters can do little about photoperiodism. But keeping tabs on changes in moonlight intensity can mean the difference between a buck on the ground and a grounded hunt. Deer are biologically equipped to respond to changing lunar periods. Consider that the illumination of a Full Moon is about the same as twilight. It can get complicated, but the latest research suggests that the first New Moon following the second Full Moon after the Fall Equinox typically overlaps peak breeding among whitetails. As one researcher described the process, "the sun cocks the [rut's] trigger, the moon pulls it." What this means to hunters is that it's now possible to time rut-phase hunts years in advance, since these lunar periods are predictable. This forms the basis for the Deer Hunters' Red Hot Rut Guide, which predicts specific rut dates for the four hunting phases of the rut over a five-year period.

Radio telemetry work suggests that deer are cued to the position of the moon, but does the moon affect the timing of the rut? If so, how?

As I said, knowing "when" can also mean knowing where and knowing how. Such as timing the high tides of activity while avoiding the neap tides. Or matching hunting tactics more precisely to each and every phase of the rut. That includes getting a grip on the best time to make amends: successfully hunting the elusive "second rut" phase. Again, this is based on the fact that, during the rut, deer don't act like Dr. Jekyll one week and Mr. Hyde the next. Quite the contrary, deer behavior changes predictably throughout the fall, much like children entering various stages of development. But before we re-examine rut phase tactics, let's re-check our data.

Researching The Rut

Any theory on the timing of the rut must be based on solid evidence. In recent times a few skeptics have suggested that the rut is not cyclical, as I maintain, but is constant (that is, occurs on the same dates each fall). Several variables--road kills, penned deer, conception dates--have been used to support this theory. Each is subject to misinterpretation, even by dedicated students of the whitetail. Consider the examination of fetuses removed from road kill does in hopes of back-dating conception dates. The basic technique of measuring the size of a fetus to determine its age--and therefore when it was conceived--is imprecise, at best. The main problem is erratic fetal growth, particularly toward the end of the cycle. This is common among warm-blooded organisms, including humans. I still remember the day I whisked my nine-month-pregnant wife to the maternity ward and blurted to the receptionist, "It's our due date." The tart response was predictable: "That date is only an educated guess," the nurse replied. "Come back when your wife is in labor." Of course Corie had been in labor for several hours and was miserable. I just used the wrong terminology to describe her plight.

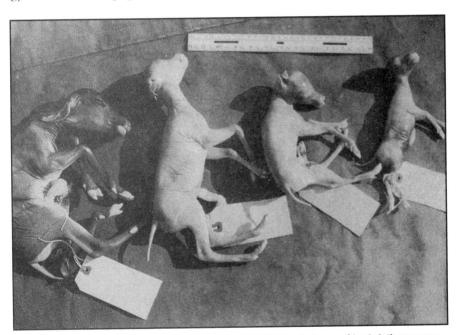

Researchers have examined fetuses, removed from road kill does, in hopes of back-dating conception dates. The basic technique is imprecise.

And so it is with back-dating road kill fetuses to reach a so-called "conception date." Even with the latest formulas, this method is a plus or minus 10 days-to-two-weeks affair. Which just won't do because that's about how much the rut varies each year. What about observations of penned deer? I certainly make it a point to network annually with several "deer farmer" friends to keep tabs on how the rut is progressing with their herds. But I'm very careful when comparing notes from enclosure to enclosure, to make sure the "biostimulation effect" doesn't skew my data. Research seems to indicate that the more contact bucks have with does, the more biostimulation--the exchange of hormones and pheromones resulting in an involuntary response--occurs and the more does are likely to cycle in a concentrated manner. Of course the reverse is also true--less contact between the sexes means a more variable and "diluted" rut cycle. So unless studies involving captivity deer control this key variable--specifically how many bucks are grouped together with how many does, and in what proximity and for how long--the conclusions are likely to be off the mark

Data derived from captivity deer can be skewed if the "biostimulation effect" isn't considered.

Academia notwithstanding, it's always helpful to know what's going on in the real world. After all, reality is reality. When I first considered how the moon's position might affect hunting tactics, I gathered harvest data from several states in the Midwest and South where deer kills are registered. I quickly discovered that success rates for the majority of days within any given lunar month were surprisingly low, and that most deer were harvested on a handful of "favorable" days. That's why the Moon Guide can be used like a report card for grading future dates--days that list Area A are better than those listing Area B which are rated higher than those listing Area C.

You can easily verify this locally. Go to any deer registration station and note how many deer are checked in during, say, a Full Moon period. Unless it's during the rut, you're going to encounter depressingly low numbers. But return a week or so later during a Quarter Moon phase, and the number of registered deer will increase appreciably. Almost always, almost everywhere. This hunter success-lunar calendar relationship isn't puzzling if you give the moon due credit. During Full Moon periods the moon is underfoot during midday and overhead around midnight, translating into more midday movement and less activity associated with dawn and dusk. Conversely, Quarter Moons are overhead and underfoot early and late in the day--when hunters are hunting hardest and when deer are most active. Makes sense to me.

I embarked on a similar path to verify the validity of my new rut theory. Besides charting rutting dates of deer raised in captivity, I compared the success rates of bowhunters and gun hunters in Illinois. Harvest data in the Hoosier State is particularly meaningful because its shotgun slug season falls in the THIRD WEEK OF NOVEMBER. If my hypothesis proves correct, the deer harvest for Illinois' opening 3-day gun weekend should be higher in years with a late rut and lower when the rut falls early. In other words, hunter success rates should be proportional to the level of buck activity. If, on the other hand, there is no such correlation, there will be little fluctuations--and certainly no pattern--in the Illinois gun harvest; the naysayers would be correct in saying the rut falls on the same dates year after year.

Well, well. As I suspected, a consistent pattern emerged paralleling the predictions of the Deer Hunters' Red Hot Rut Guide debuting in 1996-97. The Rut Guide makes bold predictions for the four main hunting phases of the rut, providing specific dates as well as unique game plans tailored for each phase. Below is the Illinois harvest record compared to my predictions published in various magazine articles as well as within the Red Hot Rut Guide:

Year	IL Gun Harvest	Change	Prediction/Reason
1994	63,014	-7%	Down; very early rut
1995	71,986	+2%	Up; late rut
1996	59,412	-9%	Down; early rut
1997	61,937	+4%	Up; late rut
1998	70,015	+12%	Up; later rut
1999	66,761	-5%	Down; early rut
2000	73,425	+9%	Up; later rut

These predictions were made public and are well-documented. For example, my rut forecast for the fall of 1997 in Buckmasters called for an increase in the Illinois gun harvest, "since rutting activity will coincide with that hunting season," I wrote. A closer look at 1998's New Moon falling on November 19 is especially revealing. It just so happens that breeding was winding down and bucks were running out of available does when the slug gun season hit. I believe the 12% increase is a reflection of accelerated buck activity more than variables such as favorable weather or high hunter turnouts. More important, this insight tells me we can take rut-hunting to a much higher level.

The real key to understanding the rut is the principle of "rut economics." Simply stated, when the demand for does exceeds the supply, hunting is best. This axiom holds water across the board, regardless of geography. Take the pre-rut, when daytime buck activity is nearing an annual peak; bucks are "primed" by alluring new odors in the woods but their makers are elusive. Only problem is, which bucks are most active, the monarchs we all dream about or adolescent bucks jockeying for position on the right-to-breed merry-go-round? The pre-rut can be good to hunters who wisely plan ahead ... but the next rut phase can be downright explosive! Too bad most hunters, never heard of it.

Remote photography (infrared sensors) at baited sights prove little; bait piles "nocturnalize" deer.

Coming to Terms

While some writers use adjectives such as chasing and seeking to describe segments, or phases, of the rut, I feel these terms are misleading and may actually do more harm than good. Fact is, during any phase of the rut some bucks will appear to be "seeking" does and some will appear to be "chasing" them around. In fact, I've arrowed bucks that were literally on the tails of does in all four rut stages.

So terms are important, and the Trolling Phase is highest on my list. It's such a tremendous window of opportunity that every sane deer hunter should learn as much about it as possible. In short, if you study the rut with an open mind and have no ax to grind, you'll discover that, from a hunter's perspective, there are actually two peaks of activity, not one. I've never seen anyone report on this phenomenon, and it's high time the hunting community gets in on it. his twin-peak discovery has remained a mystery for so long largely because it's disguised. One reason is misinterpreting the Peak Breeding stage of the rut (when most eligible bachelors have hot dates, and hunting prospects dwindle as bucks pair off with receptive does). During this phase, the supply (estrous does) exceeds the demand (dominant breeding bucks). Unfortunately, it's toward the end of a typical rut cycle and most hunters mistakenly assume the rut's over. But be at the right place at the right time a week or so later (hunting seasons permitting), and you'll see buck activity spring to life overnight. The Trolling Phase blossoms right after the does have been bred out, and it's a mad scramble for bucks to find another sex partner. So when you see a heavy-racked buck on a dog-trot in the distance, grab your binoculars and see if he's in the "troller trance." His glassy eyes, stiff gait, ruffled coat, and slobbering tongue says he's under the spell.

Formula for the Rut: 3-Year Cycle

The lunar formula popularized by the Rut Guide offers the only reasonable explanation for annual fluctuations in rutting activity. We've long known that the New Moon was a special key to the rut. Back in 1932, for instance, the federal government commissioned a study on the reproductive habits of the Indian Buffalo; from 2,457 first-hand observations of mating buffaloes, peak breeding almost invariably overlapped the New Moon. This makes perfect biological sense, as it ensures the propagation of the whitetail species. For example, if whitetails breed on essentially the same dates year after year, weather could wreak havoc with localized populations. Indeed, herds could be extinguished in some regions of the country. Spring flooding, the hurricane season, and delayed green-up caused by late-arriving springs in the snow belt are just a few examples.

On the other hand, the Full Moon-to-New Moon "cycle" ensures the rut will fall early on the breeding calendar some years, the rut will fall late some years, and some years the rut will be "on time." Early, late, middle; early, late middle. This cycle all but guarantees that during the lifetime of a healthy adult doe, at least one year-class of fawns will survive to carry on this unique synchronized breeding characteristic. It also means this neat pattern can empower hunters to cope with ever- changing whitetail patterns. Since the advent of the Rut Guide, hunters all over the nation have reported exceptional results in matching specific tactics to specific rut phases.

But don't take my word for it. Hear what brothers Mark and Terry Drury, game call experts and popular video producers, have to say. Their livelihood depends on successfully videotaping hunting scenes in the wild, and their schedules revolve around whitetail deer nine months out of the year (their only respite is targeting spring gobblers). Mark Drury is gifted with a photographic-type memory, and when I first shared my lunar theories on the rut, he spit out specific details of deer kills like it was last week. It didn't take long for him to make the "lunar connection."

Mark Drury's impressive Illinois buck, arrowed on film in October 1998, marked the beginning of his "moon-hunting" tactics.

Over the next several years the Drurys made it a point to hunt with, not regardless of, the moon. It's safe to say they're now hooked on Moon-Hunting. "We don't plan any hunts these days without first checking out [moon times]," says Terry. "[These times] are way too significant to ignore, and I think [leaving them out] is the downfall of many game plans. I've seen too many hunts, especially those revolving around food sources, turn out as predicted by the [Moon Guide]."

"Nothing always works, of course," adds brother Mark. "But the correlation between deer activity and peak lunar times and phases is becoming self-evident. I agree with Terry. I encourage hunters to consider both rut predictions and daily movement predictions in their trip planning." Riveting testimony to the potency of properly timed hunts can be seen in a new series of Drury Outdoors video productions. A good start is Walk The Walk.

Terry Drury is a firm believer in hunting both favorable lunar feeding periods and favorable moon phases during the rut.

Another key point is that rut phases are predictable to the week--and almost to the day--in the 39 whitetail states experiencing a November rut. This group includes the states of Kansas, Oklahoma and Montana which average three to seven days later than predicted dates for the other November-rut states. Five others--Alabama, Florida, Mississippi Louisiana, Texas--are exceptions to this rule and must be handled on a case-by-case basis; some geographic regions experience a December rut and some a January rut. (Texas has an October, November and December rut, depending on the area!) But even states with later ruts can benefit from annual predictions: If the rut falls earlier than normal in the "November Belt," it will fall earlier than normal in December-rut and January-rut states. It isn't voodoo mathematics.

The ability to predict each rut phase is priceless. Now, for the first time, hunters can match game-specific strategies to unique windows of opportunity. Chapter 8's introductory discussion of rut phases serves as a solid foundation.

Now it's time to build, brick by brick, on that cornerstone.

The Prerut Phase

Technically, the whitetail rut begins with the hardening-off stage of bucks shedding velvet; bachelor groups break up as dominant breeders settle into discreet "territories." This is not the easiest time to pursue trophy whitetails. We want to put the microscope on the phases of the rut that unveil chinks in a buck's armor. The first--and most celebrated--phase is the Prerut. This period is characterized by an increase in nocturnal buck movement followed by a slight increase in daytime activity. A mid- to late-October Full Moon often stimulates after-dark buck activity; bucks respond to hormonal increases with increased rubbing and scraping. Daytime activity is spurred by the first olfactory clues released by does nearing estrus.

Now here's a little secret. If you know when bucks are most likely to be rubbing trees and tearing up scrape lines, you'll also know when and where to intercept bucks: near trees scarred from previous years. So-called "multiple-year rubs" are a surefire tip-off that bucks will continue to rut in the same general areas. Naturally, sheds provide additional incentives. So plan ahead. Set stands and prune lanes BEFORE the first sign-post markers appear. Plunk your fanny and wait for rubbers and scrapers, and you could score big early in the rut cycle. The rule of the prerut is: HUNT RUBS AND SCRAPE LINES AS THEY EMERGE, NOT AFTER THEY'RE OBVIOUS.

Steve Shoop, with J & S Trophy Hunts, admires a "multiple-year rub." This is where it's at for the pre-rut.

The Peak Breeding Phase

When breeding peaks, bucks have little trouble locating receptive does. Bucks don't have to do much looking, let alone chasing, and hunter opportunities nose-dive. The problem is exacerbated in many parts of the South, where deer often exceed the carrying capacity of the land and does drastically outnumber bucks. Put another way, when bucks don't waste any energy to satisfy their mating urge, you won't see many during hunting hours. Needless to say, this renders aggressive rattling and calling tactics useless.

When bucks are paired off with does, think "isolation."

But during this fickle phase you must also alter your game plan when dealing with fairly balanced herds. For starters, the conventional wisdom of hunting high-traffic areas gets tossed out of the window. Right now any buck worth his headgear isn't about to share his female companion, so he alters his daily routine to REDUCE contact with other deer. I know it's the peak of the breeding season when I see bucks quartering does into the darnedest places--from desolate drainage ditches in the middle of plowed fields to sloughs and swamps; from brushy rock piles and isolated fence rows to dried up potholes and ponds. These are the best places to hunt, not fresh scrapes or grooved trails.

Meanwhile, a possible alternative is intercepting a buck traveling between hot does. But, frankly, this is a good time to conserve energy, bide your time, and keep a sharp eye on the rut's progression. You really want to be primed and ready for the next phase. Hence, the rule for peak breeding: THINK LOW-TRAFFIC, INTERCEPTION & OBSERVATION.

Post-rut "Trolling" Phase

My all-time favorite time to be in the whitetail woods is, by far, the short but oh-so-sweet Trolling Phase. It's a rarefied period when bucks are so desperate to locate estrous does that even Boone and Crockett-class specimens risk exposure to danger. "The prerut is okay for lots of buck action, but the trollers are what I'm after," says Mike Weaver. "These bucks can't find any more willing does, yet they're used to breeding. This combination can be the downfall of a buck that probably won't make a single mistake the rest of the year. Even though [the troller] should lay low and recuperate when his nose tells him there are no more hot females around, he isn't quite ready to give up breeding. So he trolls from one doe family group to the next." No wonder so many monster bucks are killed by hunters that never knew of their existence! I'm convinced these rogues were merely caught out of position in unfamiliar territory during the Trolling Stage.

Now's THE time to turn up the heat. Start by picking the best venues to rattle.Remember, if the wind's right, you can rattle on a calm, clear morning and let the magic sound of clashing antlers do your walking--if it's the right time, bucks will travel considerable distances to investigate. By the way, my field notes reveal a statistical advantage for mornings over evenings (3:1); the period between 8 a.m. and 9 a.m. has also been more productive than the crack of dawn.

Let me repeat: Rattling can be so effective on trollers that your entire game plan should revolve around rattle-friendly spots. The combination of elevation and funnels--to increase carrying distance and intercept corner-cutters--is unbeatable. Trollers almost always follow the terrain, rather than wind direction, when covering ground at a rut-crazed clip.

A final caveat is how to spend time. I say spend it lavishly. Most hunters are programmed into hunting mornings and evenings and resting up midday. Don't do that now. Instead, hunt hard all day. You never know when a troller might show up. Don't chance missing out. Hit the woods during this phase rested up, bring plenty of refreshments, and commit to a predawn to post-dusk vigil. So the troika for trollers: HUNT FUNNELS, RATTLE AGGRESSIVELY, HUNT HARD.

Second Estrus

The so-called second rut is supposed to hit when a subsequent wave of does supposedly enter estrus for a second time in the fall. It's supposed to be an excellent time to see trophy whitetails on the prowl again. But if theory lined up with reality, we wouldn't need all the excuses: Too cold (or too warm); too wet (or too dry); deer patterns switched (or didn't switch enough); the farmer planted the wrong crops (or harvested them too early). And so it goes with the second rut.

It's hard enough predicting the primary rut, and here we are dissecting the

You can succeed during the Second Estrus if you know how to time it.

elusive second rut. But after thoroughly researching this topic, I'm convinced the second rut is legitimate if you know when breeding peaked during the primary rut. In addition, some interesting correlations have emerged that tell us what to expect. For one, the intensity of a given year's second rut will generally be the opposite of its preceding primary rut. During a recent rut cycle, for instance, the main rut was hot for most hunters, whereas the second rut was hardly a whisper throughout much of the nation. But the following year the second rut was unusually intense--better, in fact, than the diluted primary rut. No one can say for sure why this happens, but it probably has to do with concentration levels of estrous does. Whenever a significant number of does are not successfully bred during the primary rut, more estrous does will be available the following month. This seems to stimulate aggression between bucks and may make the second rut as intense as the first in some years.

The intensity of any second rut is influenced by a trio of other factors. One is the fawn crop. In most states, fawns experience their first estrus about a month after mature does, typically mid-December throughout much of the whitetail range. A bumper crop of female fawns can stimulate sudden and unexpected buck aggression. When I see a lot of triplets, rather than twins or singles in the summer, I take note. Besides fawn-watching, observe nature: The year following a heavy mast crop usually improves fawn survival, as do years of abundant rainfall.

Second, we must factor in does failing to conceive after copulation during

In years in which the primary rut is slow, subsequent phases are usually fast-paced. When that happens, bucks like this will cut corners just as they did during Trolling Phase.

the primary rut. Ungulate research at major eastern university indicates that approximately 25 percent of female deer fail to become pregnant the first time they mate in a given fall. It's interesting to note that this percentage is higher during draught. Diet also has an impact on a doe's reproductive capacity--those animals feeding on an abundance of soft mast (see Chapter 5) and other food sources high in nutrients are going to be more fertile, other factors being equal. Third, balanced deer herds will always provide more action the second time around than imbalanced herds. In years when rut intensity is lowest, I still get favorable reports from hunters who manage to hunt blue ribbon lands blessed with a lot of mature bucks. More adult bucks during the second rut means more competition for breeding rights, pure and simple.

The main key to "second chance" rutting bucks is capitalizing on a peculiar bedding habit of theirs. During the primary rut, bucks typically relocate bedding areas: from security cover segregated from does to immediately down-wind of traditional doe bedding areas. Breeding bucks pull this stunt so they can keep tabs on estrous does and be the first on the scene when it's prime time. These "temporary bedrooms" are easy to spot, because they're punctuated with an abundance of rubs and scrapes.

Well, this predictable buck movement reoccurs during the second rut. You're on the right track if you can locate FRESH rutting sign: scraped trees with the sap still running; scrapes pungent with buck odor; and over-50-inch beds. If fresh rutting sign is hard to come by, there might be a shortage of second-estrus does. Switch to the waiting game: Set up shop near primary food sources richest in protein. Late-season does zero in on the best available food sources--winter wheat, rye and oats--and bucks won't be far behind. Meanwhile, tone down rattling sequences and rely more on tending grunts; the sound of a buck on the trail of a hot doe can be irresistible to a lusting buck ... if the demand for does exceeds the supply. So the rule for the second rut is HUNT FRESH RUT SIGN AND KEY ON NUTRITIOUS FOOD SOURCES. Just don't over-hunt these hotspots, or you'll "nocturnalize" deer and shipwreck your game plans. The rut is a helter-skelter time of year when dedicated deer hunters are as wired as the deer. Put these rules for the rut to practice, however, and you shouldn't get short-circuited. In fact, with a little luck you just might make the connection of a lifetime. ○

Mitigating Factors

The moon is not exactly a panacea for the Rut Blues. Unfavorable weather can be a disease for which there is no cure. For example, ocean patterns such as La Nina and El Nino can lead to balmy weather with above-normal temperatures and heavy doses of cloud cover. This throws each phase of the rut off, causing delays in pro-jected rut dates. Moreover, the intensity of the rut slacks off measurably when the moon is clouded over and daytime temperatures make a buck feel a guy in wool longjohns during the month of August. Bottom line: Pray for clear skies and normal temperatures for November and December!

The best strategy for hunting the rut is keeping in touch with feeding does and knowing where bucks are during the breeding cycle. The Moon Guide and Rut Guide are invaluable planners.

Chapter 10

WALLHANGER WHEREABOUTS

S o much for the when and how. *Where* are the whitetail knockouts? Two words: Near and far. Head north, head south, but don't forget the prairies. Although anybody can tag a nice deer just about anywhere these days, statistics don't lie. Here's the lowdown on where you want to plan your next vacation.

Canadian Deer, Eh?

Soon I'll be compromising my standards as I cross the northern border to hunt whitetails. Yep, I'm heading for Canada, the land of the racked giants. What's wrong with that? After all, every well-heeled trophy seeker—from the Dick Idols and Gordon Whittingtons to the Charlie Alsheimers and David Morrises—make annual treks to the land of sky-blue waters to rattle up Boone and Crockett monsters. Well, for one thing it's a big-buck proposition, all right—costs typically run $2,000-$3,000 or more. Truthfully, I enjoy hunting public lands in the Midwest with friends and family just as much (I have done so successfully for nearly 30 years; all it costs me is the price of a license, food and transportation). Besides, my home in northern Minnesota is every bit as picturesque as Canada's forested provinces.

Moreover, one must hire the services of a guide or outfitter to hunt super-whitetails in Alberta, Manitoba or Saskatchewan. Though I'm going to enjoy a pair of hunts with some folks I can't wait to meet in the next couple of years, the stigma of a guide expecting favorable press—no matter what—is not always worth the hassle. And guides can mess up.

For example, one time I hunted my fanny off with a guide in South Dakota who simply had not done his homework. He failed to make proper connections with a particular landowner who inexplicably decided to let his cattle roam precisely the creek bottoms we had hoped to bowhunt. To make matters worse, those dang cattle followed us around like Mary's little lambs, spooking deer out of cover and into the prairie (where we couldn't get close).

Now, I like the guide and continue to recommend his services to my readers.

But the episode raises a valid point: When you pay to hunt with someone, you better know what you're getting into. Don't leave anything to speculation. Find out ahead of time the basics—style of hunting, clothing needs and accessory requirements. More important, find out if the guide or outfitter is flexible. This alone could make or break your hunt. A case in point is a Canadian booking in which Myles Keller found himself hunting November hotspots in October. Myles didn't feel free to improvise, so he bit the broadhead. Frankly, Myles is not the kind of bowhunter who needs a chaperon. Just give the guy the lay of the land, and he'll finish the job. So because some provincial regulations require close supervision of non-residents at all times, I suggest you get a good handle on what you can and cannot do on your dream trip.

And what a dream trip it can be. Long before Milo Hanson's new No. 1 whitetail made Saskatchewan a household name, big-buck zealots sneaked discreetly over the border to harvest the spoils of North America's largest-bodied deer. Indeed, Bergmann's Rule decrees that the higher the latitude, the larger the homeotherm. Alaska moose are bigger than their Maine counterparts; Manitoba elk are bigger than their Colorado brethren; even Minnesota raccoons weigh substantially more than their Louisiana cousins.

These Northern giants are among the largest of 30 individually documented subspecies of whitetails, and they stand head and shoulders above the rest in two respects. Their massive surface area maintains core body heat more efficiently in the frigid zone, and a larger body consistently grows larger antlers; evidence of the impressive *mass* of Canadian whitetail racks shows up in the record books every new scoring period.

But there's another reason you should take a Canadian trip in the near future: Thanks to unseasonably mild winters in recent years, the deer herd continues to expand in many regions. And, as any hunterbiologist can tell you, an expanding whitetail herd means disproportionately high numbers of record-book animals. This is why Illinois has been hot, why some river systems in Ohio continue to grow eye-popping racks, and why Kansas is hot today.

Want to score in Canada? The boreal forest "bush" is governed by a few key fundamentals. Heed their calling and dine on venison sausage (the big ol' buck's too tough to fry, anyway), or ignore them and sip on stone soup.

• Go prepared to hunt all day, no matter how cold the weather. Harvey McDonald, with Elusive Saskatchewan Whitetail Outfitters, states flatly that deer in his neck of the woods tend to be active during middle-of-the-day hours. He cited the psychological comfort of the timbered bush that makes deer feel safer than usual during daylight hours. Then there's the comfy afternoon temperatures that give deer an added incentive to feed before nightfall. A mid to late-afternoon Moon time in Saskatchewan, where baiting is currently legal, is almost cheating.

• Forgive the broken record, but let's not forget the Moon. In light of factors discussed in the previous chapter, is it any wonder that the much-traveled David Morris, founder and publisher of *Game & Fish* Publications, meticulously schedules Canadian hunting trips around a Full Moon during the rut? It works: In mid-November 1994, he rattled to gun a dandy Boone & Crockett buck at lunchtime. Not coincidentally, on the very next day hundreds of miles away, nationally respected whitetail photographer Charlie Alsheimer rattled up a 170-class Booner, again at midday.

• Relatively few deer in wall-to-wall cover doesn't sound like very good odds. Fortunately, hunting rut sign works because of the even buck-to-doe ratio. Hang a portable along a fresh rub or scrape line, especially one situated along funnels and in strip cover. And don't forget the grunt tube.

• Discriminating bowhunters should hunt agricultural areas early—starting in late-August. (Remember Don McGarvey's Alberta monster arrowed in September.)

Check out these massive Manitoba sheds, eh.

• Rattles rub 'em the right way. It's no secret that in some camps, such as Classic Outfitters in Alberta, rattling accounts for 50 percent of bucks sighted. Find last year's rutting corridor with this year's rubs, and you might call in the buck of 10 lifetimes. Again, deer in forested regions with balanced buck-to-doe populations rely more on signpost and auditory communication than deer in agricultural lands where the herd is typically top-heavy with female deer; a surplus of does reduces competition among bucks, so what's to fight over? Conversely, does are spread pretty thin up North, and the guy walking silently carrying big rattle-bangers is playing the odds.

Put it together—good midday movement, the most comfortable time of day, the call of the mating season, the pull of the Moon—and it's airtight! Remove the Moon from the equation, however, and you'll be scratching and clawing to redeem your hunt.

So what else is new, eh?

TEXAS: SIMILAR BUT DIFFERENT

The deer population in Texas—nearing 4 million—exceeds all other states, and hunting is a $1.5 billion industry—an impressive figure compared to the $289 million hunters spend in my home state of Minnesota. Although only 80,000 archery licenses are sold annually in the Lone Star State, bowhunting is spreading rapidly. Because the state is only 2 percent public lands, most hunters belong to clubs that lease hunting rights on private ranches. Many of these lands are intensively managed for deer. You may not get what you pay for, if you don't take advantage of the Texas scene.

Larry Weishuhn needs no introduction to Texas hunters. As a former state biologist, consultant to several ranches and a frequent contributor to popular literature such as *Texas Trophy Hunters*, Larry knows "deer hunting biology" as well as anyone. When I asked him how he hunts Texas by the Moon, he didn't skip a beat.

"In many respects Texas deer are similar to [those in] other areas," he began. "Even though we don't have the lakes and streams and prolific acorn-bearing oaks that hunters typically associate with whitetail strategies, we hunt bottlenecks and funnels just like everybody else. But the ones I rely on are a little different: a unique patchwork of low-growing bushes and tall brush. It's hard to put into words, but once you get a feel for it, you'll know what I'm talking about.

"Feeding areas are a bit different, too. Almost anything that's green is considered food to deer. And while some ranchers put out bait, most of it's available 24 hours a day. So it's a lot like acorns on the ground in a big white-oak stand. In north-Texas, Spanish acorns are important, and in the brush country down South, everything is browse, browse, browse.

"My hunting strategy is fairly simple, actually. I like to hunt hard all day, even though I know that peak deer activity periods coincide with Moon position. I routinely head out before dark, and usually won't show up till after sunset unless I've got my buck.

"Down here, food sources are very important to a hunter. For instance, bucks tend to eat a lot of prickly pear [cactus] during December in one of my favorite areas. I think it's because [the cactus] is fairly palatable, high in vitamin A and carbohydrates. And it's pretty succulent, providing much-needed moisture. In some areas bucks—not all of them, but certain individuals—will continue to return to the same clump of prickly pear to feed just about every time they pass through the area. They do this year after year. Find one of these clumps that's been eaten down and you can set up a tripod [treestand] and wait them out or rattle, if the timing is right.

"As I said, I find that my most productive rattling occurs when the Moon's up. I've called in way more bucks at this time; when the Moon pulls [on a buck's] instincts to fill his rumen, he'll be up and moving and more inclined to investigate the sound of antlers. So I'm definitely mindful of those peak times and I always try to be in key areas when they occur.

"Stillhunting areas I know hold bucks, based on the frequency and size of rubs and scrapes, is a good way to work myself into position, especially if the peak feeding times are, say, midday or early afternoon. If there's something out there deer really like to eat, so much the better. And, by the way, water can be critical in Texas, too. We're blessed—or cursed, depend-

Larry Weishuhn, one of the country's original Moon hunters, with one of eight bucks he killed in 1994 (next time you see Weishuhn, ask if he's had a "falling out" with Robert Goulet).

ing on your point of view—with highly fluctuating water levels. This turns some stock dams and ponds into a food plot of sorts—when water levels recede, the perimeter sprouts with tender forbs. If the Moon's right and surrounding cover is adequate, big bucks are apt to water and feed right on schedule [with the Moon].

"Stillhunting, glassing and sitting periodically all work in conjunction with predictable habits of Texas whitetails. Another thing: Hunting out of a vehicle is legal in Texas. I'm not talking about 'road hunting' here, but extensive use of a 4 x 4 to quickly eliminate unproductive areas."

"What throws many non-resident hunters off," said Bob Zaiglin, "is the diverse habitat of Texas. Eastern Texas is quite similar to the Southeastern United States—some hardwoods, some pine stands. The [central] Hill Country is a smattering of dense thickets—scrub oak, juniper, dense shrubbery—in a rolling, broken landscape. Farther north, it's basically grown up antelope country: mesquite, scattered hardwoods and brushy draws. Here, forbs are especially important.

"South Texas' famous brush country doesn't have the forbs, but with all the nutritious browse, the deer don't need it. Finally, the southeast coastal region, the King Ranch area, is mostly sandy-loam soils where deer subsist more on forbs and less on browse species. So it's a very dynamic, changing environment you must become familiar with to hunt properly."

What food sources do bucks seem to prefer? According to Zaiglin, the number-one choice of the brush country's successional stage growth is Granjeno, which is 21% crude protein. Also: lime prickly ash (an aromatic, thorny bush), LaComa and acacias legumes (nitrogen-fixing plants high in crude protein).

"Bucks can bed and feed in the same area because of all the cover," Zaiglin said. "However, shade in the semi-arid region is critical, and persimmon and taller-growing plants are important for preventing long-distance movements during heat-of-the-day periods."

OK, besides feeding and bedding areas, what about transitional habitat? "Bucks bed up in the thickest country we have for protection from coyotes," Zaiglin said.

Jerry Johnston, publisher of *Texas Trophy Hunters*, thinks that the "lunar effect" is the hottest topic in the whitetail world since rattling.

"When deer move, they feed along the way, so their 'transition zone' is also a feeding zone. They have an inner bedding area and an extended transitional feeding zone, because the brush country's forage species are so abundant and varied that they enhance [the deer's] nutritional opportunities. These bucks are not dependent on hardwoods or grainfields with all of the nutrient-rich browse."

A final key to Texas is fresh rain following a drought. Natural regenerated forage—brand new terminal shoots—are preferred by deer over anything, including corn, Zaiglin says.

A Prayer For The Prairies

A recurring nightmare has plagued me for about 25 years. My wife thinks it's hilarious, but the dream is so real I often wake up in a cold sweat. Ooh, I'm shivering at the mere thought of it, as I recall the details:

I'm before a judge, having been cited for some sort of game violation. (One time it was having too many arrows in my quiver; another time I was charged with hunting too many states in the fall; still another time I was hauled before the court when a virused computer declared my license number null and void. The details change, but the theme remains constant: constant haranguing by the law.)

"Well?" asks the judge, leaning over a shiny oak bench.

"Well, what?" I ask.

"I'll have you in contempt of court, if you smart off one more time like that," he snaps. "Well… how do you plead?"

The words roll off my tongue without me having any control over them. "No contest, your honor. I'm not guilty. I mean, this law isn't…"

"You can't plead no contest *and* not guilty," the judge interrupts. "Make up your mind."

Fumbling for politically correct words for this most delicate of moments, I respond, "What I mean is, your excellency…"

"Guilty!" the judge declares, slamming a gavel in my camouflaged face. "I'll teach you to flatter me. Excellency, huh? I sentence you to…"

At this, a hush falls before the court. Babies stop crying, toddlers quit fidgeting, the bailiff no longer jingles keys in his pocket, even the court reporter stops reporting.

"I sentence you to one," the judge continues, pausing for effect, "and only one habitat to hunt deer for the rest of your life. Well, Mr. Murray? Speak up now. Which shall it be?"

One habitat? Gee. Does he mean what I think he means?

Fingers tap loudly on oak veneer, first the pinkie, last the forefinger. "Well?"

"That's easy, Omnipotent One," I say. "I'll take the prairies. You know—Kansas, southern Minnesota, Nebraska, the Dakotas, Texas, Colorado, Manitoba, Saskatchewan, Alberta…"

As absurd as this sounds, I got off easy. Whitetails are fun to hunt anywhere—from the deep woods of Maine or Minnesota to a Georgia beanfield or a Kansas wheatfield—and the prairies top my list. Three reasons:

First, prairie deer are large-bodied animals compared to other subspecies of whitetail deer, and therefore grow impressive racks. The *dakotensis* and *texanus* subspecies account for a disproportionate percentage of record-book racks (the *borealis* subspecies is close behind).

Second, whitetails often reach full maturity in open, largely uninhabited spaces of the prairies, and this, along with genetics and nutrition, is a prerequisite for growing impressive headgear. (Speaking of nutrition, the nutrient-rich soils of the prairie make it the breadbasket of the world.)

And third, hunting the prairie environment is never dull. You get to see lots of deer. Prairie deer occupy a unique niche in the whitetail world, one that presents uncommon opportunities and obstacles. Joe Admire, a soft-spoken outdoorsman from Tulsa, Oklahoma, has studied these deer for 30 years. Here are some "admirable" tips:

- Get the jump by scouting in late summer when deer are bunched up and feeding contentedly in the open. The mature, dominant bucks break timber and feed in fields. Alfalfa is their top food choice, and you'll see a lot of big bucks because they typically bed in draws several miles away to distance themselves from roaming cattle and ranching operations.
- Open the season between feeding and bedding areas (during a favorable Moon). This is how I arrowed that Nebraska eight-pointer I mentioned earlier. "Take a stand on the edge of the cover so you can see which trails the bucks are using and which ones the does are sticking with," Admire says. "Then you can glass and hunt at the same time."

One important footnote: Some prairie seasons don't open until October. Roll with the punches. "One September morning I saw 13 Pope and Young bucks in a particular coulee," Admire says. "But by the time the season opened, they'd vanished. When October rolls around and acorns begin to fall, the deer completely change their patterns. They file into the draws and coulees that are closest to oak stands. And bucks become nearly nocturnal at this time. You probably won't see a single book buck until the first does go into heat." (Incidentally, a typical prairie

Hunt the prairie like Oklahoman Joe Admire, and you might nail a buck like this one that netted 166 2/8.

125

diet preference goes like this: alfalfa, beans, sunflowers, milo, corn and winter wheat.)

Bucks In Your Pocket

Jim Hill has a few good bucks to his credit, thanks to the prairie country of southern Minnesota and the eastern Dakotas. Here are a few pocket pointers:

- Come prepared to "scramble around like a coyote," as mentioned earlier. Hill thinks most bowhunters blow it on prairie deer by not maintaining a super-low profile. Sew knee pads on your trousers. Get used to looking for sand burrs and other prickly plants (to know the sting of pain is to belly-crawl over a toy cactus.)

- To avoid being made out by sharp-eyed prairie deer, take a hard, close look at your outer garments. Hill agrees with Myles Keller that most camouflage patterns are too dark; they show up as a distinct "human blob" on the landscape. Patterns that work well for conventional treestand hunting usually won't do out on the flats. Backland (All-Terrain) is surprisingly effective as is Realtree All-Purpose Grey.

- Develop a glass eye. Hill, like Myles, typically spends days on end just watching for deer to take the same route a couple of days in a row. "Once you bump deer in the sparse cover of the Dakotas and southern Canadian provinces, the bucks will exchange brushy bottoms for open hills," Hill says. "They'll bed where they can wind you from behind yet spot you a mile away. You're cooked."

- Look for patterns involving potential ambush points. For example, prairie white-tails tend to follow "structure" from point A to point B—a dimple in the land-scape, a fenceline or a tree or two. When a buck passes near a certain geo-graphic landform more than once, Hill says, you better take note.

Especially keep the element of surprise on your side when hunting out-of-the-way pockets, Hill says: "Most of these deer have never seen a human in this stuff, and that's why they hole up out here. If you're sneaky, you can score."

Noted last words from a notoriously sneaky guy.

- Now, forget about bucks and key on does. "What does do in October is pretty much what they'll be doing during the rut," Admire says. "The bucks are into the same basic routine, often bedding in close proximity to one another, but again, you just won't see them. They're beginning to set up rub and scrape lines near the concentration of does." For the first time, bucks become territorial; so if you monitor individual doe groups, you can keep in touch with the bucks.
- By the end of October (sometimes the first week of November), buck groups totally break up. You'll see individual animals in the search mode, and if you've done your homework as explained, you could be in for a treat. This is the time period that Admire and his son, Joe Jr., recently arrowed three Pope and Young bucks within a week. "It's as good as it gets," the studious bowhunter maintains.
- During the rutting peak, hunting can be decent, but luck can work against you. For example, Admire believes that when a mature doe goes into heat, a dominant breeding buck has "first rights" in the pecking order. Because does bed predictably in low pockets at night where air currents settle—providing the safest zone for deer—a buck has little trouble locating her. He'll lead her away

from the rest of the herd to avoid competition from rival bucks. This occurs mainly at night for about seven or eight days in a row; the buck will probably breed four or five does during that time.

This goes on largely unnoticed, and it often "takes place out in the prairie, away from the cover" you're hunting, Admire says. While the rut "can move deer into your lap, it has a way of working against you."

How true. While hunting with Bird-n-Buck Outfitters during the 1993 rut, I found myself in the same stand Joe Jr. had taken his pair of Pope and Young bucks 10 days earlier. Though I had three nice bucks within bow range in three days of hunting—and I saw another half-dozen in the distance chasing does—the deck seemed stacked against me. Every buck zoomed through my area in pursuit of a hot doe. Close but no Havana. So:

- If you don't score on a big buck in early November, your best bet during the rut is simply waiting it out. "Don't do anything foolish such as wandering off for greener grass. Or hopscotching from stand to stand," Admire says. "You'll only end up telegraphing your presence. Be patient." Hunt hospital clean, and play the wind by setting up several stands to cover a hot area like the back end of a stock dam—a classic Oklahoma funnel (ditto for an elbow or bend at the base of a steep wall).

- Hunt hard from Thanksgiving to Christmas. The key is making two factors work together—a shortage of breedable does and predictable feeding patterns. The first period occurs immediately following the peak of the rut. Bucks take chances when searching for late-estrous does; for a week, maybe 10 days, big bucks have had their way, but not now. So they go looking instead of waiting. Be smart and set up where bucks can look for does most efficiently.

"Late-estrous does like to bed in thickets near the rims and edges of coulees, not down in the timber," Admire says. "I've watched bucks work these thickets just like bird dogs, sniffing out patch after patch. When they find a receptive doe, the two pair off and disappear."

In some years, you won't see many big bucks in this search mode, but in other years they seem to be fairly common. Environmental factors such as drought and storms may be chief influences on how "spread out" the breeding season becomes. So is the timing of the New Moon.

Elk in Light of the Moon

Elk are basically oversize deer. In fact, hunters who consistently get close to whitetails will have no trouble scoring on bull elk… provided they negotiate one itsy-bitsy teenie-weenie detail: Finding the critters.

Elk differ from deer mainly in how they're distributed. Whereas you'll find deer scattered fairly evenly throughout their range, elk typically concentrate in micro-areas—a herd here, a herd five to 10 miles away, and so on. Needless to say, prime elk habitat is big country, and differentiating this week's hot drainage from last week's leftovers takes some legwork! On top of this, everything looks elkish to the untrained eye.

The starting point? Take some sage advice from Bob Todd, with California's Department of Parks and Recreation. When you first arrive at your destination, contact fish and game or Forest Service field workers. "They're usually quite happy to point you in the right direction," Todd says. "This [suggestion] has saved me invaluable time on out-of-state hunts to Idaho and Oregon." One time Todd called a conservation officer who was recommended to him by an acquaintance from another unit of government. Again, it saved miles and days. So don't be embarrassed. Call those whose jobs put them in the field on a regular basis.

Topo maps are an invaluable aid. For example, look for drainages with steep contours along creeks and bottoms, then scour the immediate area for benches described earlier; the contours will widen, indicating a flat area along the moutainside. These are ideal bedding areas, and could be the hub of elk activity.

One more tip before getting into Moon strategy. Weather affects elk and elk hunting a great deal. Briefly, in years of dry weather, water becomes the key to the hunt. Meaning, elk will inhabit lower elevations because they can't get enough moisture from grazing; they will visit "drinking areas" and bulls will wallow up a storm in the excessive heat that typically accompanies drought conditions. Wet weather, on the other hand, tends to drive elk higher up the slope, and the herds will be scattered—lush vegetation proliferates throughout their range and isn't limited to south slopes and creek bottoms.

Now that you're up to your ears in elk, here's how to use the Moon. First, avoid Full and New Moon periods, if possible. During these portions of the lunation, morning and evening elk movements near open food sources—where they're most easily glassed and vulnerable—are suppressed. On the other hand, sneaky stillhunters might enjoy the prospects of pussyfooting through lodgepole pine, closing the gap on a regal bull that's trailing with cows nibbling on browse during midday. Full and New Moons are made for stalking sideslopes and bedding areas in the black forest.

Which isn't a bad idea, especially for mega-bulls that let the satellite bulls and raghorns do most of the bugling and carousing. Take a cue from Arizona bowhunter Jay Elmer. When he's in his new-world-record mode (a mark he once held with a remarkable 389 ²/₈ bull), he doesn't sit over a water hole. He doesn't bugle, either. Rather, he "ambushes" bulls. By knowing the lay of the land and where a spotted bull is likely to end up, Elmer relies on honed stalking skills to

Elk are just big deer. Use the Moon Guide™ system to predict when and where they'll be feeding, and you can intercept them.

close the gap. He stays with the bull as long as it takes, until everything is just right. Then and only then does he close in.

Sound familiar? Indeed, this is the way Myles hunts, including the time he arrowed his 6x6 Pope and Young bull, which was the largest elk taken in Colorado with gun or bow in 1974. He'd spotted the buster and tagged along with the herd until he could slip an arrow into the bull's chest from close range. It took days of clawing and scratching and sleepless nights relocating in the dark.

Long ago *Outdoor Life* hunting columnist Jim Zumbo told me that if I wasn't heading out from camp in the dark, I'd surely miss out on the best time to catch elk before they retreat for heavy timber. From a decent vantage point glass meadows and openings with high-power binocs or a spotting scope, he said, and note precisely where the elk enter cover. If they aren't disturbed by the time you get to the spot, they should be within a half-mile of where they were last seen.

What about bugling? Like rattling, it's all a matter of timing. Bugling elk elicits an aggressive response, and you won't find much of a correlation to the Moon and bull rutting behavior (except for a New Moon overlapping cool weather). The best handbook on bugling elk, by the way, is, appropriately titled, BUGLING FOR ELK, by Dwight Schuh (11959 Winther Ave., Nampa, ID 83651; 208-466-0343). The only rap is this book's in its 14th printing, and Schuh has learned a lot about elk since compiling this edition. (Hey Dwight, how 'bout an update?) On the other hand…

An ideal situation is when a bull has collected an impressive harem, and they're feeding by the Moon in thick cover. Elk are not that difficult to sneak among because they make such a racket as they plod along. A sneaky elk hunter who sets his watch to the Moon time(s) of the day has a definite edge: He knows when elk are most likely to be taking nourishment. He just might be able to sandwich himself between the bull and a few "wandering cows."

Another scenario is hitting prime times—when the Moon's overhead or underfoot near dawn and dusk. Perhaps the easiest time to kill elk might be when they're in a predictable feeding pattern—early and late in the fall. Purposely time your trip to avoid lunar periods that preclude elk from feeding in open parks and coulees early or late in the day. Then do a lot of glassing from above, and cut them off at the pass. If you make it a point to pack as far back as your legs will carry you, odds increase, because elk will continue to feed by the Moon. Otherwise, you'll be battling hunter pressure, which always impacts daytime big-game movement.

ABC's of GPS

GPS stands for Global Positioning System. For you cave-dwellers, GPS played an instrumental role in the overwhelming success of Operation Desert Storm, and now civilians can take advantage of this incredibly precise military guidance technology; relatively inexpensive hand-held units are commonplace in sporting-goods outlets across the nation. The more I fiddle with this whiz-bang contraption, the more my devious mind does cartwheels. For example, I can:

- Never get lost, not even where magnetic interference foils my compass.
- Use the plotter screen on my Eagle AccuNav, which shows current position in relation to point of origin (and destination, if known), to return "blindly" to camp after dark.

Keith "Teeth" Kavajecz wouldn't have gotten this nice mulie without his Eagle GPS

Dennis & Mary Stickney
PO Box 581
Sumner, MI 48889-0581

- Store as many as 200 waypoints (a fancy term for places of special interest), giving each a unique name for remembering and retrieving months or years later.
- Keep my bearings in rugged country, navigating deftly around dangerous rock rims and bluffs—again, in the dark, if need be.
- Exchange information with fellow hunters, saving time and legwork. (For example, my friend Doug Tryon knows the exact location of three elk wallows in southern Colorado, and all I have to do is compute their coordinates from a topo map and punch them into my GPS unit.)
- Retrieve wounded game by examining the network of "plot trails" on the screen of my unit to look for pockets that have been overlooked. (Plus, I can return the next morning, picking up exactly where I've left off to resume tracking duties or pack out the animal.)
- Help save a life—if a buddy breaks a leg or snaps an Achilles' tedon, I can probably locate him faster than a local Red Cross chapter.

GPS units can be intimidating to those raised and educated prior to the video age. I suggest making a waterproof copy of the operating manual and toting it along at all times. Play with the unit back home until you're familiar enough with it to navigate confidently where you've never been before. (The backcountry is no place for first-time GPSers.)

Be sure to pack along about five times as many backup batteries as you think you'll need (the AccuNav consumes AA batteries like my teenaged son dines on chuck steak). I'm exaggerating a wee bit, but you certainly don't want to leave the unit running on its fastest update mode. A wise accessory is a cigarette lighter adapter that lets the unit determine its current location without draining battery power (it takes time to triangulate your position from several satellites orbiting the Earth). When you first arrive at camp, set the unit on the hood of your vehicle and let it initialize itself.

My friend Keith Kavajecz, a former computer programmer, loves his AccuNav, but another buddy, John Powers, found his Magellan Trailblazer to be more user-friendly. Prices are coming down, and although I continually draw the line on the encroachments of technology in the hunting world, I can't imagine hunting elk—or deer, for that matter—without topo maps and a hand-held GPS. Find a model you can get comfortable with, and here's betting you'll be partners for life.

Are Bears Moonstruck?

The guy on the other end of the line was frantic. When's my Moon Guide™ going to be shipped? he asked. Seems he was in the planning stages of a big bear hunt up north, and he wanted to know when he could expect to see the most boars over bait. I tried explaining that the Deer Hunter's Moon Guide™ is designed for ungulates—animals with chambered stomachs that must feed in cadence to the Moon. But he didn't want to hear it. Which got me thinking. Do Moon times apply to bears? Or turkeys? Bighorn sheep? Moose?

After more research than I care to admit, my answer is maybe; no, yes, yes. Bears are crepuscular and they become nocturnal only when human pressure forces them to hit the graveyard shift. Yet my notes reveal an amazing correlation between bear sightings and afternoon Moon times. In view of the fact that bears are predators and therefore are used to "feast and famine" feeding forays, I suspect this phenomenon is linked with the natural tendency of predators to be

131

active when abundant prey is most active.

In other words, thousands of years of this predator/prey relationship might have taught bears to be on the prowl when deer—a principal food source in the spring and early summer fawning period—are most active. That makes a pair of daily lunar periods of at least casual interest, wouldn't you say?

Regarding turkeys, they don't know where they're going till they get there. And when a spooked gobbler lights in a tree, he stays out on a limb until he forgot why he flew up there in the first place. This is not to say turkey hunting is a snap. Duct-tape binoculars across your forehead, and you might be able to see as well as a gobbler. Or saddle up with an ostrich and you might be able to keep up with a flock of Merriam's. But track them by the Moon? I doubt it. Unquestionably, their biological clock is circadian—they roost by night, feed by day. A midnight Moon time won't pull them off their roost.

Sheep and goats and moose and possibly caribou are another matter. All are ungulates, possessing chambered stomachs designed for alternating periods of feeding and rest. Migrating caribou might respond to environmental factors—they've got somewhere to go before the elements turn against them—more than lunar forces from time to time. But I'll never head for camp without my Moon Guide™. The Moon's universal pull affects everything from clams to man. Certainly ungulates. O

132

Big ol' bears, like this 20-inch Saskatchewan boar, might be on the prowl during the fawning season when deer are most active...

Handsome bucks like this tend to "hang up" just out of bow range. Why?

CLOSING THE DEAL

n the good old days, when I'd catch a glimpse of a nice buck slinking along just out of range, I had four options at my disposal: I could wring my hands; clench my teeth; hold my breath; or try striking a deal with the Almighty ("Lord, steer that buck my way, and I'll be home for Christmas."). The grunt call and modern rattling tactics have added a couple more arrows to my quiver of tricks, but I'm still dealing with too many shoulda, coulda, woulda hunts. Rattling, in particular, unnerves me. No other hunting tactic produces as many close shaves that start out rosy and end up dismally.

Take the buck I once rattled within three paces of my treestand (seems like yesterday). He circled directly behind me, and I didn't know he was there until I heard him grunt. A tree limb obstructed a good view of his rack -- not to mention a clean alley to his chest -- so all I could do was hold my bow at half-mast and wait. Would that I drew right away! His massive 10-point rack, bobbing up and down in the brush as he trotted away, would have easily put him into the Boone and Crockett record books! But it was too late to get the draw, let alone aim for a killing shot. Another close shave.

If I had it to do over, I'd certainly do some things a bit differently. It's all about closing the deal, a subject I've become intimately familiar with of late. Subtle refinements to the game of calling and rattling deer can close the books on many accounts.

Grunt Gumption

Although a few hunters and some Indian tribes have been calling deer for more than a century, the so-called grunt call era blossomed in the 1980s. Larry Richardson's paper, "Acoustics of White-tailed Deer," published in the Journal of Mammology in 1983, sparked much of the fire. Richardson documented seven different sounds after recording them with sensitive microphones and analyzing their "sonograms" with a sophisticated instrument, the Spectograph. In 1988,

Tom Atkinson with the University of Georgia published his findings on the subject in the American Midland Naturalist; at least 12 different vocalizations were reported. From a pure hunting perspective, the grunt -- particularly the "tending grunt" -- emerged as the call with the greatest in-the-woods potential.

David Hale (left) and Harold Knight (right) have helped pioneer the commercial grunt tube. Larry Richardson started it all with his paper, "Acoustics of White-tailed Deer," published in 1983.

We've come a long way since verifying that this call is worth taking along on every deer hunt, and in spite of its overuse hunters continue to score on bucks that would have otherwise escaped untouched. Still, I believe we can tweak the grunt call's overall effectiveness, especially for luring bucks those few extra critical steps. The starting point is picking a call with the proper pitch.

The first generation of grunt calls all sounded pretty much alike and were improvisations of reed-type duck calls (a plastic reed vibrating against a hollow chamber when blown gently). Eventually manufacturers learned better ways to mimic the pig-like grunt of a buck tending a receptive doe. Some designs proved to be better than others.

Producing the Moonbeams video series taught me this valuable lesson a few years ago. It all crystallized for me in the wee hours of a marathon editing session when I was trying to "sweeten" the sound of a distant grunting buck. (With mixers and software programs it's often possible to modify the audio track to make subtle sounds more distinct.) It took about a dozen passes to get it right, and that's when it struck me: The typical buck grunt in the wild isn't nearly as guttural as many commercial models make it out to be. In fact, a real grunt is comparatively sharp and piercing--like running a finger across the teeth of a large comb, only a little deeper.

I couldn't wait to test a raft of makes and models with my production company's sophisticated audio equipment to see which ones compared most favorably to the buck on film. After-hours sessions turned up a fistful of calls that my ears liked the best; however, my sound technician wasn't convinced, and he brought up a good point. "I think you're hearing what you want to hear," he said. "I can't tell that much of difference, and I'll bet the deer can't either." He might have been right about my ears, but it would boil down to how well deer can hear.

The sound frequency of whitetails is only 500-12,000 Hz, but by pointing each ear in a different direction, a deer can measure the difference in time it takes for approaching sound waves to reach each lobe. This allows them to pinpoint specific sounds with surprising accuracy.

137

An Earful of Advice

Research indicates that a whitetail's brainstem response to pitch (sound frequency) is only 500-12,000 Hz, while a human's range is closer to 20-20,000 Hz. But deer have learned to make up for their less sensitive auditory system. The net result actually gives them the edge in hearing perception. I got a graphic illustration of this during an encounter with a Northwoods buck that looked as big as a moose.

A light rain had dampened my spirits that day, as my waterproof-breathable raingear was proving to be more breathable than waterproof. Just 15 more minutes, I thought to myself as I watched the intersection of two trails below my treestand in a towering white pine. Suddenly I got one of those sixth-sense sensations that told me to check my backside. I slowly turned my neck like a snowy owl as I kept my body statue-still. Sure enough, there, behind a big blowdown, stood a barrel-chested buck with a thick, chocolate-brown rack. For the longest time he didn't twitch a muscle, and I thought I might be hallucinating. But my heart began to race when I noticed his breath in the cool, damp air.

He was only two paces from a clear shot, but that's a huge distance when a buck decides to hold his ground until he's good and ready. Would you believe that, over the next 30 minutes, neither one of us didn't move an inch? What a sinking feeling it was to climb down my treestand in pitch dark, wondering what happened to the buck. To make matters worse, to this day a hitch in my neck reminds me of that painful incident.

But the lesson was a valuable one. I firmly believe that that buck was relying on listening skills. In fact, he never raised his nose to test the air. Perhaps his instincts told him that the steady rain would restrict the movement of odor molecules that evening, or that odors wouldn't carry as they normally would. Whatever the reason, the buck seemed to know that his ears were a better front-line defense than his nose.

Make no mistake, deer can hear. If you could swivel your ears like a whitetail, you could make a comfortable living with Barnum & Bailey, as deer ears can pivot 270 degrees. They function like sonar. By pointing each ear in a different direction, a deer can measure the difference in time it takes for approaching sound waves to reach each lobe. This, in turn, allows him to locate the source of specific sounds with surprising accuracy.

Armed with this knowledge and a fannypack stuffed with an assortment of grunt calls, I experimented on every deer I saw over a four-month stretch. While most calls produced intermittent results and none were foolproof, a handful of models proved more effective than their competitors. Because specific models come and go, depending on sales and not necessarily on productiveness, I'll share the manufacturers: Hunter's Specialties, Primos Hunting Calls, M.A.D. Calls, and Knight & Hale Game Calls. Again, to a casual observer most commercial grunt calls sound alike, save for loudness (more below). But I'm glad I took the time to compare apples with apples to avoid a few lemons. The main point is, if deer are consistently hanging up just out of range, your grunt call might sound more like a mallard than a whitetail. Find a better one.

Always grunt louder if a buck appears to ignore you and grunt softer the closer the buck gets.

Once you get your hands on an authentic-sounding call that produces the sharp treble (not muffled bass) we're looking for, learn how to use it wisely. Let's rehearse a few do's and don'ts:

- ★ Do call if the buck is losing ground and losing interest.
- ★ Do call LOUDER if the buck appears to ignore first attempts.
- ★ Do call SOFTER the closer the buck gets.
- ★ Don't call if the buck is looking your way.
- ★ Don't call if the buck is gaining ground or appears interested.
- ★ Don't call the same way (tone, duration, intensity) every time.
- ★ Don't call when in doubt.

Keep in mind two additional pointers. First, no grunt call is worth a hoot if bucks can't hear it. That's why I always carry a "magnum" model with an extra-large sound chamber. It may sound a little "quacky" up close, but it really reverberates in the woods and gives me the extra carrying distance (up to 75 yards) I need to turn a distant buck. It's more of an attention-getter call (what the heck was that?) than a true lure call (where's that buck?). If you don't have time to switch from the former to the latter, be sure to muffle the sound with your fingers for up close coaxing.

139

Second, the tending grunt that simulates bucks in hot pursuit of does isn't the only call worth buying; two other calls also merit strong consideration. The so-called snort-wheeze is a sound that rutting bucks make when they're unusually aggressive. This doesn't happen very often, so don't overuse this "lure of last resort." M.A.D., by the way, makes an excellent one. And the so-called aggravated grunt, that ranges from a "bellow" to an elongated ticking sound, should also be part of your repertoire. An economical option is one of the new "variable" models that allow for adjustments to the call's pitch during operation. Some even produce a tonal range high enough for bleats.

Several game call manufacturers suggest that whitetails converse in a language as complex as humans, necessitating a myriad of calls to handle a myriad of hunting situations. While whitetails do "talk," I believe it's misleading to say they engage in dialogue. The calls discussed above should suffice for most hunting applications, with the possible exception of the doe bleat. This is an excellent long-distance attention-grabber for bucks, because its exceptionally high pitch pierces the woods particularly well. But a bleat's not going to transform you into the Pied Piper of Whitetaildom. And neither will a grunt call; nothing's magic and nothing always works. Still, if you blow the wrong call or make the wrong sound, you could blow -- not close -- the deal.

Rattling: Quality Counts

Hunters must first put themselves in the Red Zone if they expect to score, meaning rattling can be a waste of time if you don't do your homework. For starters, always hunt balanced deer herds. We've noted that the lower the doe-to-buck ratio, the more competition among bucks, and the more "differences of opinion" will end up escalating into head-to-head combat.

Southern deer herds are notoriously unbalanced, with does typically outnumbering bucks by as much as 10:1 or more. At first glance, this is not the best place to rattle in a record-book buck. According to the Pope and Young Club, Florida ranked 46th on the list of record entries with only six. South Carolina placed 43rd with 17 typical Pope and Young entries. Discounting Texas' 10th place (449), and the in-between "midriff" states of Kentucky (13th; 307) and Virginia (21st; 151), we're left pondering: Arkansas (24th; 110), Mississippi (25th; 101), Georgia (26th; 100), Tennessee (29th; 70), Alabama (30th; 68), and North Carolina (33rd; 59).

Billy (left) and Rusty (right) with sheds proving it's possible to grow big bucks down South.

But statistics can be misleading. Times are changing. Thanks to educational efforts of the Quality Deer Management Association (QDMA), headquartered in Watkinsville, Georgia, many southern states have adopted regulatory changes that are beginning to alter the antler landscape. Consider that "harvestable" bucks must now have: At least eight antler points or be at least 15 inches wide in a six-county area in Georgia; in Mississippi, at least four antler points; in Arkansas, at least three antler points on one side. Further, in Tennessee the buck limit was reduced from 11 to three. And new regs in a tri-parish area in Louisiana implemented a six-point antler minimum while liberalizing antlerless deer harvest options.

So hunting's getting better in the South. A few falls ago, I found my thrill on a hill in South Carolina. The folks at Wildhaven enrolled 2,000 acres of prime whitetail habitat into a stepped-up deer-management program. The Shannon boys, Billy and Rusty, are smashing the notion that all whitetail bucks below the Mason-Dixon line are stunted and runt-racked. The key to growing braggin' bucks down South is elementary, they insist: Keep does in check, whittle down the buck population of 8-pointers, and let the 10-or-betters dominate the gene pool. Based on a quick week of bowhunting, I'd have to say the boys are doing just fine. For more information, contact Wildhaven, Rt. 3, Box 425-B, St. Mathews, SC 29135; 800/239-9951.

This fine South Carolina buck I took during my stay at Wildhaven debunks the theory that you can't rattle effectively below the Mason-Dixon line. You just need balanced deer herds and rattle-able real estate.

Meanwhile, good rattling ground in the Midwest, where the Borealix and Dakotensis subspecies are known for producing impressive racks, is getting harder to find. To begin with, hunting pressure on public lands has escalated as private land access has dwindled in recent times. A chief contributor is the environmental movement. Nature-loving non-hunters relocating to rural areas have been deceived into thinking they can "preserve" wildlife; they post their lands and wall off hunters. Meanwhile, numerous "coalitions" funded by left-of-center foundations, such as the Pew Charitable Trust and the Turner Foundation, have effectively stifled rural economies: Logging, agriculture, dairy farming, mining, and ranching have especially been targeted. Most of these landowners used to welcome hunters but now many depend on "trespass fees" to make ends meet.

Then there's a serious access issue spawned by the "wilderness society" crowd. Numerous NGOs (non-governmental organizations) are working behind the scenes to "unmanage" forested tracts by designating mulitple-purpose areas as permanent wildernesses. A key component of this movement is closing off roads and trails, such as the Clinton Administration's roadless campaign affecting 60 million acres of federal land. An unfortunate side-effect is increased hunting pressure; limiting access concentrates, rather than spreads out, where hunters can go.

One solution for dealing with this trend is the Hunting Club. Enterprising hunters pooling their resources can lease ground managed primarly for hunting and secondarily for other activities such as farming, logging, and ranching. What does this have to do with rattling? Everything. Rattling in quality whitetails in a quality habitat is but a pipe dream if you don't critically analyze every potential hotspot, whether or not you pay for hunting rights.

Rattle-able Real Estate

As I strive to refine my hunting techniques over the years, one thing I've learned the hard way is that not all hunting ground is created equal. It's a cruel joke that two seemingly identical parcels can produce disparate results. While they may both host the same number of deer, including mature bucks, one will usually be more rattle-able than the other. You need to know what to look for before you leap, and it doesn't matter if you're dealing with Scotland County, Missouri; Pike County, Illinois; Buffalo County, Wisconsin; or Dooley County, Georgia.

For example, in spite of rattling's considerable carrying distance--up to several hundred yards--it's pointless to rattle where bucks can't hear you. It should go without saying that you need to pick a spot where bucks are likely to hang out during hunting hours. But this flies right over the head of many hunters. Stated simply, there are only three places you can rattle--where deer feed, where they bed, and travel corridors connecting the two. Which type of habitat should you be concentrating on?

The best place to rattle is a travel corridor. Why? Because confining serious rattling sessions to where bucks are likely to be on their feet will bring more dingers to the bell. Chapter 8's Full Moon tactic of rattling the cage of bedded bucks is often necessary because of the number of "C" days (bedding areas) the Moon Guide predicts in a given lunar month of 28 days. But if you get a chance to rattle on a "B" or "A" day, you'll be dealing with more daytime buck movement. Here's the secret: For some reason bucks on their feet are more responsive to rattling than those that are bedded down. It seems that once a buck curls up for the day he gets into a bunker mentality and survival dominates his thinking. You might be able to tease him within hearing distance, but coaxing him those critical extra yards will be tough.

Next, narrow down travel corridors where natural funnels and terrain features constrict deer traffic. It's a familiar tune, no doubt, but I've seen a lot of hunters make two critical mistakes. Either they waste time over "hot" buck sign that's typically associated with a buck's bedding area, or they try to set up where the terrain is relatively featureless. Hunters should spend the extra time looking for a spot where bucks are likely to be coming and going rather than settling for low-percentage areas.

A shortcut might be the "corner-cutter." Regardless of the time of year, bucks will take the quickest route connecting their destination and point of origin. Start by determining where bucks and does are bedding -- they never bed together with the exception of a buck tending an estrus doe -- and slip in between. Exactly where depends on the topography. Conspicuous terrain features always shape the way a buck is likely to travel. It may be a steep bluff or a river bend; the head of a deep hollow or a ridge point; a saddle on a knoll; or the edge of a swamp. Sooner or later a buck skirting one of these features will show up on his way to a hot date. Less-distinct features can be equally effective: ditch crossings, dips in a field, beaver dams, and the like.

The corner-cutter becomes my top priority when "rut economics" comes into play. When the demand for does exceeds the supply, you can count on accelerated buck movement. It's a wonderful time to plop down at a key spot and let the bucks come to you.

An interesting exception is deliberately setting up shop near traditional doe bedding areas when the Rut Guide predicts that the prerut is about to unfold. "Doe bedding areas are taylor-made for the prerut," says Mike Weaver. "Bucks get tired of waiting for does to come into estrus, especially when only one or two have cycled in a local herd. Bucks hate to miss out, so they scent-check each doe bedding area in their terrritory to see who's hot and who's not. Sometimes a buck will even kick does out of their beds to get a better whiff. If you've got stands placed in the right spots, you could see action any time of the day during this stage [of the] rut."

I've successfully rattled in bucks on opening day, during the rut, and just after the rut when a blanket of snow covered the landscape. While timing is important, the better the spot, the better the rattling. When evaluating prospective hunting areas, make a list of these key components to rate their true potential.

Rattling Basics and Beyond

Now that you're in position to score, it's time to call the right play. Before we get to rattling's best-kept secret, here are the ground rules.

Always rattle:

* ⋆ Regardless of the calendar period, not just the during the rut.
* ⋆ Aggressively during the rut, particularly during the prerut and the post-rut "trolling" stage when competition for breeding rights is keen.
* ⋆ Conservatively if you find yourself dealing with a lot of adolescent bucks; one of these juveniles could peg you and blow your cover.

Never rattle:

* ★ For "the heck of it" (expect results and be prepared to shoot at the drop of a hat).
* ★ At a buck facing your direction.
* ★ At a buck that's traveling toward you.

How skilled does one have to be to effectively counterfeit a pair of bucks butting heads? In my opinion, technique is over-rated with two glaring exceptions.

An incident that occurred while hunting with J & S Trophy Hunts in southern Iowa proved to me that technique isn't everything. I'd timed the rut just right and managed to score on a nice 10-pointer in spite of unusually hot weather that severely restricted daytime whitetail movement. One evening in camp a hunter complained about "another guy setting up too close" who was "rattling too often." I had a hard time swallowing the notion that my friend, Steve Shoop, would compromise any hunter's chances (Shoop has earned my respect as the best in the business). So I jumped into the conversation.

"Are you sure it was a hunter rattling and not real bucks fighting?" I asked.

"Damn sure," snapped the hunter. "The guy was using [a set] of those cheap imitation gizmos--ya know, made out of plastic."

"How could you tell?" I persisted.

"It was easy," he insisted. "They sounded hollow and tinny. Besides, [the guy] carried on all morning long. Bucks don't do that."

Well, that hunter was dead wrong. I spared his ego by not telling him I was the closest hunter to him and that I'd glassed a pair of bucks fighting off and on from dawn to nearly noon that morning. So the question begs, if this guy can't discern the real thing, how can he reproduce it?

This anecdote raises another point that costs hunters opportunities for closing the deal: When the rut's on, they don't rattle enough! Scrap the conventional "wisdom" that says too much rattling will "give your position away." Rattling is a natural sound during the breeding season, and deer know it. Besides, bucks are incapable of reasoning, "Hey, there's too much fighting going on around here; must be hunters trying to fool us." If you're going to rattle, RATTLE.

If you're going to rattle, RATTLE. And be READY.

On the other hand, there's a lot more to rattling than smacking a pair of main beams together. In fact, when I rattle, I mostly grind. Surely you've heard stories of bucks "locking up" for extended periods (each year bucks fight to their deaths because they couldn't unlock). Fact is, when bucks go head to head, they mostly push and shove and shake their heads. This is precisely the sound we want to imitate most, not merely the initial crack of antlers making contact at the beginning of a heated contest. So make sure GRINDING is the main goal; twist those antlers against each other instead of banging away.

In spite of all of these precautions, chances are you'll still end up rattling in a buck that circles in the thick stuff or hangs up short. This is especially common for bowhunters, with their limited effective range. After mulling this over for nearly two decades, I've concluded that the cause and the cure are one and the same. According to Pope and Young statistics, about 80 percent of all record-book bucks are taken from treestands. While it's hard to argue with the benefits of an elevated position--unequalled visibility, superior scent control, improved carrying distance for calling--this tactic hurts rattling as much as it helps.

Here's why rattling from a treestand is often a good-beginning, bad-ending proposition. When a buck picks up on the racket, either he closes ground quickly or circles cautiously. But many times your position above the ground prevents the buck from pinpointing your location. So he pulls up short a "comfortable distance" away as he evaluates what he thought he heard while waiting for additional clues. Sure, a timely grunt call might help, as alluded to earlier, but what the buck really wants to hear is the fighting sound of rivals squaring off.

Let's make sure we know this is fact and not supposition. Three reasons explain why the sound of cracking and grinding antlers consistently attract bucks like no other in nature: 1) During the rut, bucks instinctively know hot does are often part of a fight scene; 2) early in the fall, before hunting pressure puts bucks on the defensive, curiosity is a natural response; 3) about a month after the primary rut, bucks contend aggressively for a limited number of "second estrus" does. Add it all up, and it all adds up: When stuck in neutral, all a buck wants to hear is MORE RATTLING.

My slick trick of jangling from a treestand is sure to close the deal more often than not.

But this is impossible, you say, as any movement will surely tip off the buck. Not necessarily. You've made a good pitch, and now it's time to close the deal. The solution, however, requires a willingness to stake the outcome on a novel rattling technique that seems risky at best. I call it "jangling." Specifically, I'm talking about aggressively clanging together a pair of antlers suspended from a rope below your treestand . I first heard about it from Mike Weaver, who perfected the technique from years of experimenting on mature bucks. "Without jangling," he confided, "four [of my] Pope and Young bucks would have certainly gotten away. They were on a half-trot when they did a complete 180 and ended right in my lap." Indeed, when you pull a Mr. Bow Jangles impersonation, it gives a buck something to zero in on, and he often bolts on a dead run straight for your treestand.

Naturally, considerable caution and forethought are necessary for handling standoffish bucks. For example, I've learned the hard way that I better stow my antlers at the base of my tree rather than hanging them on a tree limb at arm's reach. By tying a rope to my treestand so the antlers dangle at ground level, I can reach over unnoticed and give them a timely yank without suffering detection. And timing is always critical. Just as the best time to grunt at a sighted buck is when he swings his head, you want to jangle just as the buck is about to head out.

An Illinois bruiser fell for this tactic recently. The symmetrical 10-pointer tiptoed cautiously toward me about 15 minutes after I'd rattled hard for a minute or so. In fact, I was considering a second session when I first laid eyes on him. Predictably, he froze about 75 yards out, so I tried a seductive grunt when he wasn't looking. No interest. I waited until he took his next step before I grunted a second time. Again no interest. But when he turned to leave, I yanked on the rope and jangled as hard as I could. Whamo! A few leaps and bounds put the buck right below me facing my direction. After a brief standoff, the buck hopped into a thicket that was, well, too thick to shoot through. Though it was another close shave, I squeezed two extra chances out of the encounter. That buck was lucky ...

When you're trying to drum up some buck business, always start each session from above. But when you're done, always return the antlers to the ground rather than the other way around. In fact, I typically conclude each rattling session by letting the antlers free-fall with a crash landing. I can't prove this triggers more bucks, but I know I've rattled in a lot of them since I adopted this ritual.

In addition, it's a good idea to add the sound of rustling leaves to the sounds of clangin' 'n' bangin'. Gently bounce the antlers against the forest floor, rolling them over dried leaves, sticks, and grass. Another ploy is unleashing more rope and casting the antlers 15 feet or so off to one side. Then drag them back before more jangling. These extra sounds tossed into the mix can really make a difference at times. Simply put, they're what a buck expects to hear when he thinks rivals are squaring off in the distance.

Grunting and rattling are the most effective aggressive tactics available to modern hunters. While they aren't complicated or difficult to master, they're easy to use incorrectly. But these new wrinkles will help even the score and close more deals. ◯

JURY-RIGGED FOR RATTLING

This seven-step program is a sure cure for Post-Rattling Depression:

1. Start with a medium-sized pair of main beams; a rack that would score about 120 Pope and Young inches is about right (any smaller and the sound won't carry far, any larger and the sound might be too intimidating to other deer).
2. Saw off the brow tines. They'll only get in the way and could cause injury. Likewise, remove unessential non-typical points, and file down the burrs at the base of the main beams to prevent chafing.
3. Drill a quarter-inch hole, just above the pedicle, through both main beams.
4. Cut a heavy-duty polyester cord about three feet long and thread it through both holes. Tie a pair of double-knots at each end to prevent slippage.
5. Tie a loop in the middle of the cord with a simple overhand knot (the loop should be about one inch in diameter).
6. Cut a rope to length–at least 10 feet longer than necessary to reach the ground from the height of your treestand. Secure one end to the above loop with a pair of half-hitches and cinch the other end to the seat of your treestand; knot it up where you can reach it without looking down.
7. Always start each rattling session from above and stow the antlers at ground level between sessions.

Be sure to tie the knot so there's enough space for the antlers to jangle together when suspended from a rope.

147

Chapter 12

WHEN THE GAME IS ON THE LINE

W ith these strategies destined to put you on top of game, your scent better not give you away at the moment of truth. Join the unscent revolution, and you've nothing to lose but your fatty-acid chains.

The Unscentsation

A plethora of scent-elimination products has evolved in recent years, competing fiercely for hunters' dollars. But are they a slick advancement… or the product of slick advertising? I mean, is it humanly possible to not smell like a human?

Until recently, I didn't think so. None of the dozens of concoctions I field-tested kept deer from blowing the whistle on me. No matter how religiously I bathed, sprayed or smeared, deer hung up predictably at the 50 to 75-yard mark. Still I kept bumping into credible hunters—guys with no stake in a scent company's bottom line—who claimed to beat a buck's nose. Here's the latest scoop.

The Science Of Smell

Odors are a collection of volatile molecules, gasses wafting in the air. It takes a nose—a unique apparatus endowed with olfactory receptors and neurons—to detect scents and a brain to interpret the information. The process remains one of life's great mysteries, and scientists are just beginning to explore the many roles odors play in the animal kingdom.

Way back in 1953, Dr. Walter B. Shelley and his associates proved that the peculiar smell of man is largely the result of bacterial action on sweat produced by apocrine glands. He also proved that sweat is sterile and therefore odorless in the absence of bacteria. Meanwhile, research on deer has shown that their keen sense of smell is due to a nasal cavity richly endowed with innumerable and various kinds of receptors, and a brain that's about three-quarters dedicated to the perception and evaluation of odors. No wonder a whitetail's sniffer can pinpoint and age a particular scent source by measuring minute differences in the number and location of triggered receptors!

Too bad we can't just "hunt the wind." Myles, who helps spread the Gospel of Unscent, according to Scent Shield, is right when he says trophy animals have an ingrained habit of circling perceived danger. "Man's the top predator in the food chain," he says. "Get rid of your scent, and hunting becomes fairly easy." Easy for Myles to say.

Louis B. Johnson, a microbiologist and chemist from Alabama, "hasn't been winded in a half-dozen years." A few years ago, Jim Hill arrowed a South Dakota buck approaching from downwind. And Kansas trophy bowhunter Lynn Leonard told me he watched his then-14-year-old son, Travis, arrow a fine Pope and Young mulie from a direct, downwind line.

Nevertheless, for every hunter who's achieved unscent nirvana, thousands of skeptics scoff at the notion. The fine line separating the two camps, I now believe, starts with an all-or-nothing commitment. "You can't just spray away and expect to get away with murder," says Ambush's Tony Newman. "You have to be a fanatic. Then when you pick a product with good chemistry behind it, you'll get results."

Mask Or Masquerade?

Before the concept of odor neutralization caught on in the late 1980s, most hunters went under cover—so-called cover scents, particularly fox urine and skunk, were dripped and draped on boots and trees to "mask" human odor. "It doesn't work, because deer are capable of detecting multiple odors at the same time," insists Johnson, who cleanses himself with the B-Scent Free line of products he began marketing in 1988. "Heck, one minute my bird dog can get sprayed by a skunk, the next minute [she can] root out a covey of quail."

On the other hand, some herbal cover scents seem to help considerably, claims Dr. James C. Kroll. Contradiction? Not necessarily. It isn't practical to eliminate *all* body odor, but a conscientious scent-control routine can reduce the count to *trace* levels. And that's where the aromatics and herbals come in: apples, juniper berries, bayberries, cedar sprigs and pine. Pungent, naturally occurring odors can confuse deer when body odor approaches "threshold levels" (defined as the lowest concentration required to be perceived). Perhaps this is why predators such as cats and canines instinctively roll in a rotted fish or carcass when given the chance.

You don't have to be a rocket scientist to figure this out, but in the case of Dr. Una Lynch, it doesn't hurt. (She earned her Ph.D. in chemistry with her work on rocket fuels and converted that knowledge into an all-out chemical warfare against odors.)

"To detect methyl alcohol, you need 5,900 ppm [parts per million] but only .000000032 ppm to smell vanilla," she began. "Guess which one's easiest to mask? Obviously, some odors are more difficult to disguise than others."

This is sure to upset the scent-control apple cart. Consider a recent Iowa bowhunt with whitetail fanatic John Hambleton, who challenged my rubber boot theology. Each morning before the hunt, Hambleton rubbed smashed apples across his *leather* hunting boots. I was convinced deer would pick up his trail and backtrack out of my hunting area, so I mentally marked his comings and goings. Unbelievably, every deer intersecting his apparent scent trail totally ignored it!

"Rubber isn't the best choice for hunters," agrees Dr. Lynch. "[It's] the perfect environment—dark, warm, moist—for growing bacteria and fungi that stink up the feet. Worse yet, once the odor builds up, it eventually passes through because rubber is gas permeable, even though it's waterproof. Don't forget, odor is a gas."

Will this buck wind you if he circles downwind?

Odor Neutralizers: Good Chemistry

The joke about the Finlander disappearing when he tried Odor Eaters has a grain of truth to it. One reason modern hunters can reduce their odors to trace levels is that the latest batch of hunting products strikes at the core of the problem: They deal with the source of odor, namely, the dirty work of bacterial compounds (technically low-molecular fatty acids) that deer find so alarming.

Today's scent-neutralization revolution actually began in 1974 when Dr. Una Lynch coined the phrase "No gas, no odor" and introduced a line of products designed to control pet odors. Once Dr. Lynch determined the chemical compound of an odor, she figured she could alter it. Which is how Ambush, a company she consults for, works on human odor: It neutralizes the acids created by bacteria, forming non-volatile solids (typically salts). Ambush is the only patented neutralizer, and its principal ingredient is a stable form of bicarbonate (not baking soda).

Scent Shield's Bill Robinson pioneered this basic concept in the hunting world. Robinson was a salesman with the company that Lynch worked for, and he purchased the pet division inventory and hired a chemist to adapt the formula to the hunting community. Scent Shield was first introduced at the 1986 SHOT show and was all but ignored. "'Laughed at' is more like it,"

The scent-neutralization revolution is for real.

Robinson says. "But I knew it was perfect for hunters, so I refused to give up."

Back then I interviewed an obscure bowhunter by the name of Myles Keller who discretely mentioned a "spray bottle" that allowed him to "get within five feet of a pair of does." Robinson and Keller later joined forces, and interest in Scent Shield skyrocketed overnight (fights reportedly erupted over limited supplies in some bow shops).

Other manufacturers—at last count about 50—soon followed. Louis B. Johnson's B-Scent Free, for example, boasts a triple-action formula. First it kills bacteria on contact, then it prevents regeneration by increasing the pH (from about 6 to 11.5, a level Johnson considers optimum to check bacteria without causing skin irritations). Finally, B-Scent Free leaves a fine, powdery film that catches odorous gases that might escape from the body through clothing.

If you want to know which neutralizer's best for you, conduct a simple experiment. (Research by Dr. Yas Kuno revealed that, due to diet and genetics, BO varies from individual to individual.) Economize by teaming up with hunting buddies, each purchasing a different brand. Then trade and compare notes. Bottom line: If you can smell a hint of BO after application, a deer can easily detect you. Keep looking for a spray that works. When you find one, reapply often (the warmer it is, the faster bacteria colonize).

More Technology

Some companies take a different chemical route to achieve scentlessness. Oxidizers (N-O-DOR) destroy the odor molecules the way chlorine functions in a swimming pool. And oxygen scavengers (Odor Free) bind up oxygen around the odor-infected area to produce odorless carbon dioxide. Industrial odor elimination—big business in the sewage industry—has seeped into the hunting market, too. One product relies on enzymes that reportedly gobble up odors.

Doctor Juice Odor-Lok combines anti-bacterial action with a principle borrowed from modern surgery. To "lock up" viruses, fungi and bacteria in operating rooms, a particular ingredient is applied to keep microbes from releasing into the air. Odor-Lok is heavy on that ingredient.

Powders are ideal for gloves and boots, particularly in cold weather. This generation of products based on "molecular sieve" technology holds some promise. For example,

A sneaky Jim Hill rummages through his scent-proof pack for a Scent-Lok carbon-activated hood. Hill has helped convince me that the product is a technological breakthrough, enabling bowhunters to negotiate wind-shifts and swirls like never before.

"abscents crystals" have a negative ionic charge that causes odors to stick (adsorb) to them. Just as important, the unique shape of the crystals gives them a tremendous capacity—one teaspoon reportedly has the surface area of a football field. B-Scent Free Powder and N-O-Odor II employ the principle of adsorption, which is why carbon works so well.

And how. Southern Minnesota bowhunter Mike Kohler discovered that Scent-Lok is for real when he removed the hood of his carbon-activated suit while crouching 15 yards downwind from a mature doe. "Prior to that she fed contentedly," Kohler said. "Then within 15 or 20 seconds she bobbed her head and stomped her feet. She must have been badly fooled because she snorted for the next 150 yards. That's when I knew [my suit] was no ordinary scent system."

Scent-Lok's carbon nodules, impregnated evenly into the fabric, are nondiscriminatory about which odors they trap. Whereas most commercial sprays work best on acids, carbon catches all foreign odors. Even so, my initial experiences with Scent-Lok were unscentsational—deer kept winding me. But I now realize hunting without the hood was a huge mistake (it reduced my hearing, but I've since cut slits for my ears). Scent-Lok has boosted performance since first-generation products by laminating carbon between two protective layers of fabric.

Conscientious scent-control is an important part of hunting with J & S Trophy Hunts.

Beyond BO

The human body emits odors from vectors other than apocrine glands. These odors are not as offensive, but they must be addressed by hunters:

- The palms of the hands repel deer like amino acids repel fish, thanks to butyric acid concentrations detectable to the human nose at .00028 ppm (parts per million). When in your hunting area, wear Scent-Lok gloves or those sprayed with an odor neutralizer.

- Feet stinking like Limburger cheese are the result of bacteria and fungi. Soak toes in a mild solution of water and bleach and keep the toenails clipped and clean. Also consider exchanging rubber boots for breathable footwear that's properly stored. (Jim Hill sticks with rubber boots, but he stores them year-round in a tight-lid Rubbermaid container filled with dirt and fresh oak leaves; the boots absorb the earthen odors.)

- Bad breath can blow deer away. Researchers at the University of London discovered that dogs could be trained to apprehend criminals strictly by the unique smell of their breath. Gargle with vanilla, munch on parsley sprigs or don a Scent-Lok hood.

- Scentlessness is only skin deep. Dead skin cells pile up around your blind or tree-stand as the epidermis continually "sloughs off" tiny granular particles rising to the surface from the dermis. Neutralize the skin, and stuff pant legs inside socks or boots and sleeves inside gloves.

- Pilling is almost as bad. Fabrics continually break down, transporting your scent along with airborne microscopic "lint." Choose a pill-resistant material (cotton is one of the worst, Dacron is one of the best).

- Never dry hunting garb in a contaminated dryer; after showering, dry off with a towel washed in unscented detergents. Use special unscented lubricants for guns and bows.

Incidentally, to reactivate a carbon suit, simply load it in a hot drier ancycle for about 45 minutes.

The goal of scent-control is preventing deer from bolting. "A buck's olfactory system is a 'closed loop,'" maintains Greg Sesselmann, inventor of Scent-Lok. "When he senses danger, his knee-jerk reaction does not involve any reasoning. He smells, he bolts. However, if hunters can reduce their scent to trace levels, deer will most likely reach a different interpretation: Either the hunter will appear to have passed through the area earlier, or will seem farther away than he really is. The perception of more time and distance gives the deer a cushion—and hunters a big edge."

Since its introduction, I've been a fan of Scent-Lok. My reasoning is simple: ANYTHING a hunter can do to reduce his scent stream is going to pay off. Simple mathematics tells me that even if I can't totally eliminate all human and foreign scent emanating from my body, the less distance my scent carries, the more bucks will end up in my lap. In recent years Scent-Lok has greatly improved their product line, making it more durable while boosting its scent-trapping capabilities. It isn't perfect, but it's the closest thing to it.

Control BO? No Sweat

When a deer winds you, it flees in terror as it smells a mixture of chemical compounds—low molecular fatty and hexenoic acids—multiplying on your skin. Here are some key facts about body odor that could help in deer camp:

- Bacteria are micro-organisms, called flora, that feed on sweat excreted by apocrine glands on the skin of adults (babies have no body odor). These glands are located under the arms, back of the neck and knees, and on the forehead, scalp and pubis. The body also excretes sweat from 3 million eccrine glands, distributed throughout the body, but this sweat is odorless in healthy humans. Translation: Concentrate on the apocrine glands.

- Drs. Albert Kligman and Najib Shehadeh discovered that odor from the pubis is not due to bacterial action (apocrine glands present did not secrete apocrine sweat), but from excreta. Translation: Moderate cleansing, not scrupulous anti-bacterial hygiene, is sufficient following urination or defecation.

- Scrupulous hygiene, however, is critical for controlling BO in the armpit and scalp area. Research by Switzerland's Ashley Cox showed that long-term use of the anti-bacterial agent Triclosan (registered under Irgasan, sold by Ciba-Geigy) has a cumulative effect. Other research proved that scrubbing arduously (a minimum of two minutes) with an effective anti-microbial agent can make a significant difference.

- Oily hair follicles, associated with the sebaceous glands on the face and scalp, are a fertile environment for odor-producing bacteria. A simple solution is cutting off the bacteria—literally. Japan's Dr. Yas Kuno noted that females smell less than males and Asians do not smell as much as Blacks and Caucasians. Shelley and cohorts proved that shaving armpits helps greatly, and the same probably goes for beards and ponytails.

- Bacteria require an incubation period to produce BO, so contaminated clothing should be washed with a detergent containing a bacteriostat such as Triclocarban.

- Hunters need a concentrated deodorant that's odorless (different from unscented). A pair of products boasts "chemical synergism" (the result is greater than

the sum of the effects taken independently). B-Scent Free's Extended Wear Deodorant is composed of two flowers, Calendula and Arnica, originally pioneered by the Israeli military and subsequently modified to eliminate residual odor; it lasts up to a week. Robinson Labs' Body Shield Gel, an unscented lotion, combines two powerful ingredients with an Aloe Vera base that helps soothe dry skin, occasionally brought on by scent neutralizers.

- If you can't shower or your water supply is limited, try N/R Laboratories' No-Rinse Shampoo, reportedly used by astronauts on NASA flights. Just towel dry after massaging the shampoo into the scalp (no rinse needed). Several companies market anti-bacterial towelettes, too.

It all sounds good to me… and to my wife. Even though I may still come home skunked, at least I won't return smelling like one. In fact, these days I smell pretty unscentsational.

The Cold War

Too many hunts are over before they get off the ground because hunters can't take cold feet. Sooner or later you're going to face Old Man Winter—an anti-hunter if I ever saw one—head on. When he throws the landscape into the deep freeze, you've got to win the Cold War—from the ground up. Basically, hunters get cold because they choose the wrong boots and the wrong underwear. I aim to change that:

Born and raised in Duluth, Minnesota, I know the dull ache of frozen feet as well as anyone. So did Mark Twain, who wryly commented that the coldest winter he ever spent was a summer in Duluth. But purple toes and tingling feet are largely a figment of the past for the Murray family. We don't get cold feet anymore because we don't have to—modern boot design all but eliminates frostbitten feet.

Hydrophobic (water -hating) materials combined with low-loft, high-efficiency insulation offer the best of three worlds: They're dry, warm and lightweight. The Gore-Tex/Thinsulate "sock" option is vastly superior to earlier generations. Cabela's unique Mountain Hunter II, imported from Italy, is a testimony to how the boot design pendulum has swung—stout hiking boots have given way to ultralight jogging designs because bulk and weight are no longer needed for strong support (or warmth). Weighing in at a svelte 3.4 pounds per pair, these boots proved worthy of their name during a cold spring outing. With relative ease, I negotiated rugged Merriam's turkey country in spite of blizzard conditions. A Gore-Tex liner, 200 grams of Thinsulate, AIR 8000 lamination over 1,000-denier Cordura and an impact-absorbing urethane midsole make this boot a top contender for rugged terrain.

Cabela's Mountain Hunter II boots are lightweight, waterproof and surprisingly nimble.

About 80 percent of Americans

157

complain that both of their boots don't fit well. The reason is that relatively few of us have matching feet. If yours are really out of conformation—unusually slim, fat or flat, with fallen arches, bunions or hammered toes—you're a strong candidate for a custom job. This may seem expensive, but it's quite economical in the long run. Ten years ago, for example, I purchased a pair of chukka boots from a professional bootsmith and, although I'm on my third sole, the stitching remains completely intact. The W.C. Russell Moccasin Co. (285 W. Franklin, Berlin, WI 54923-0309; 414-361-2252) continues to crank out—make that hand-craft—custom boots to fit customers who send the company measurements of their feet (according to catalog instructions). Established in 1898, Russell is a trusted name in custom footwear relying on moccasin construction (a continuous layer of leather around the foot). The boots come single, double or triple "vamped."

These boots are for moderately cold conditions. When it freezes, you need to step things up. I do not recommend felt-lined pacs, because they trap moisture and hold it next to the skin. Another problem inherent with "wool" felt liners is that the customer never knows what he or she is getting. The base material is essentially reprocessed wool, but is typically blended with other materials—often cotton—to reduce cost and help the liners retain shape. And the more cotton used, the less wicking occurs and the quicker your feet get cold.

You can remodel your old pacs by replacing the liners with the Sun Walker made by Trophy Glove (122 Washington Ave., Albia, IA 52531; 800-323-2928). Comprised of super-high-loft lamilite, these liners not only lighten up the boots but enhance their water repellency. Also, be sure to add a comfy insole. (Freelonic, 63 Grove St., PO Box 169, Salem, MA 01970; 617-744-0300). Or consider a boot with open-cell liners like Red Ball's Quad Pac. A total of seven different types of insulation go into the Quad Pac—three in the liner and four in the outer boot.

Looking for super-warm, comfy undies? My vote goes to Patagonia's Expedition Weight Capilene.

When it's frostbite freezing, one boot design particularly stands out. Chimo, which means "hello" in Inuit, could help say good-bye to cold feet. The Chimo Boot sports a cleated, soft rubber bottom that's vulcanized (not sewn or glued) to a nylon upper shell. The liner is a doubled 100 percent wool duffel sock. Beneath the sock lies a three-quarter-inch felt insole, and beneath that is a unique nylon Saran mesh insole that serves as a "frost trap" (remove it each day to rid it of ice crystals). The boot laces loosely around the foot, and it's a little bulky at seven pounds. But do you want warm feet or not? (Totem Outdoor Outfitters, Ltd., 7430 99 St., Edmonton, Alberta, Canada TGE 3R9; 403-432-1223.)

Underwear has come a long way since the days of itchy woolies. What you lay against the skin has a direct bearing on how you can stand the cold. If you will be fairly active, any wicking undergarment such as Thermax or Blue Johns will transfer moisture from the body and keep you optimally warm. But if you expect to be motionless for hours on end, the warmest underwear I've tested to date is Patagonia's Expedition Weight Capilene. The loft of the velour-like fabric traps air with its brushed inner and outer layer, and it's very comfortable, because it stretches proportionately with your body angles. (Patagonia, PO Box 8900, Bozeman, MT 59715; 800-336-9090.)

With good boots and undies, quality outerwear should keep you plenty warm. The Raven Wear Polar Fleece anti-freeze system, particularly the vest and sherpa-lined bibs, is among the best. (Raven Wear, Box 411, Caroline, Alberta, Canada TOMOMO; 403-722-3896.)

Finally, don't blow it by eating all wrong. You need a diet that's designed for energy release while stoking your furnace. It's so simple: Combine high-fat foods that burn slow-but-hot with lower-burning foods that are quickly metabolized: Buttery oatmeal for breakfast; carbohydrate snacks throughout the day; high-fat meals at night. Compare this with the guy chowing down on high-protein steaks. And when he guzzles coffee, it's no wonder he'll be caught with his pants down (caffeine blocks a hormone that restricts urination).

When you finally get the draw, will you draw a blank?

Beating Buck Fever

Though it was an Indian summer afternoon in October, my friend Tom shook like a homeless dog in January. His kneecaps danced as if they were leaning against an electric fence. His heart raced out of control; his fingers and toes tingled. As an avid deer hunter of many seasons, Tom was used to the nervous excitement that accompanies the sighting of a buck—it's what keeps him coming back for more.

But this time was different: Tom could breathe in but not out. When the eight-pointer stopped broadside, 15 paces away, Tom didn't get off a shot, let alone make it count. Thanks to oxygen buildup, he was too dizzy to see straight. And instead of feeling euphoric, he felt nauseated—his lungs, now pregnant with air, pushed painfully against a queasy stomach.

Buck fever strikes again! It can hit anyone, anytime, anywhere. Neither beginners, nor veterans are immune from an attack. Bob Foulkrod, veteran guide, outfitter and promotional hunter, knows this as well as anyone. Pick up a Golden Eagle Archery catalog or visit an authorized dealership, and you'll likely see Foulkrod's cold, confident pose above a huge Saskatchewan whitetail. Don't let it fool you.

"I had that buck at 10 yards and couldn't draw my bow," he said somewhat sheepishly, shrugging his shoulders. "All I can say is, I was lucky to get another shot."

Not everyone gets a second chance, though. Like one of Foulkrod's clients during a rigorous caribou hunt in Quebec. For several days the duo kept up with thundering herds stretched out across the rolling tundra. "We could get close enough to smell them, but we couldn't close the gap," Foulkrod said. "It was classic bowhunting: frustrating but fulfilling."

Then it happened: A regal bull "close enough to see the veins in his eyes" suddenly popped up at spitting distance. The bowhunter drew his bow and released an arrow. Well, sort of. Buck fever saw to it that the confused archer released his bow and hung onto his arrow! "The bow whipped back and bounced off his chest," Foulkrod explained with a wince, "catapulting toward the surprised bull."

Buck fever is especially tough on elk hunters. When pitted face to face with bugling bulls, human behavior can be as unpredictable as the animals. Take the New Jersey gun hunter who missed a huge 6x6 bull inside 50 yards five straight times. After the smoke cleared, the bull stood untouched and began heading toward the wide-eyed hunter. He went bananas. "He's going to kill me," he shrieked, tossing his rifle down like the bad guy in a Hollywood flick.

But deer have mesmerized more gun hunters over the years than any other game, and they show no signs of letting up. John Weiss, a nationally respected deer author, got "roped" into a buck fever session about five years ago. He still hasn't fully recovered. "It had been a long fall," Weiss said. "I hadn't seen a single buck, even though I bowhunted hard on my tree farm every day. Now I'm down to the next to the last day of the shotgun slug season, and I'm real desperate."

Weiss didn't see or hear a thing that bitter cold morning, so he decided to head home for lunch and warm up. After unloading his trusty Remington pump, he lowered it below his stand with a long rope. Just as it reached the ground, a light stamping noise in the leaves caught Weiss' attention. He turned to find a somewhat bewildered eight-pointer staring up at him. "Like I said, I was pretty desperate," he continued. "In hindsight, I should have froze until the buck looked away, then lifted the gun a foot or so at a time. But I flat out panicked, hauling the gun up hand over fist as fast as I could." What happened next is textbook buck fever: Weiss got the gun to his lap all right, but he couldn't shoulder it. He was literally at the end of his rope as a big loop wrapped around his gun and several coils around his waist. By the time he managed to free himself, the buck was long gone.

A gun's safety mechanism is a favorite target of buck fever. Outdoor writer Kathy Etling rediscovered this timeless truth one frosty November morning when she joined her husband, Bob, at his stand to soak up some heat from his portable Coleman propane heater.

"Bob figured two was a crowd, and he decided to let me hunt his stand," Kathy recalled. "No sooner had he hit the ground when I saw a big buck crossing a sight lane. 'Bob, there's a huge buck over there,' I whispered. 'Over where?' he asked frantically.

"Well, I pointed over my shoulder, and Bob still couldn't make out the buck. Eventually he saw it and got off a shot. When we found the nice 10-pointer Bob was ecstatic. 'Oh, honey, you're so wonderful!' he exclaimed. 'How many wives would let their husbands shoot this buck instead of taking it themselves?'"

Not many, including Kathy Etling. Truth be known, in the excitement she kept shooting with her safety on. Bob was lucky to beat her to the draw. Better thank buck fever, not Kathy, for that trophy whitetail, Bob...

Sometimes buck fever doesn't kick in until after the shot. One time my cousin Jerry Larson shot a thick-necked buck from his stand in a forked popple tree in northern Minnesota. In his heightened state, he defied gravity and jumped all the way to the ground (about 12 feet) to claim his prize. And speaking of jumping, I personally know a guy whose "rifle jammed" so he jumped on the back of a whitetail passing beneath his stand. And I also know a magazine editor who was all smiles after downing an impressive whitetail... but I had to wait for him to quit vomiting before I could take his picture (the photo is priceless).

Buck fever has a few ugly sisters, including, but not limited to flinching, flock-shooting and target panic. The latter can ruin a dedicated bowhunter in a single season, giving the afflicted fits when trying to draw, aim and hold on a target. During a recent stretch, for example, outdoor writer Michael Pearce missed the same Kansas Pope and Young buck four times; a big Colorado bull elk at point blank range; and a handful of other trophies. At one point, Pearce became so downtrodden that when a nice buck appeared in the distance, he secretly hoped it would stay out of bow range.

Now that you realize you're not the only one coming unglued at the moment of truth, here's what you need to know to keep yourself together.

First, confront the problem: Buck fever is a mental *and* physical phenomenon. At the sight of an impressive rack, what sane hunter doesn't experience a quickened pulse and a heightened awareness? The "rush" is caused by the release of stress hormones such as epinefrin secreted by the adrenal glands, located at the top of the kidneys. This God-given response, known as General Adaptation Syndrome (or fight or flight syndrome), is actually designed to negotiate times of stress. But for many individuals, self-control is lost when the mind works against, not with, the body.

The rush of adrenalin may be unavoidable; however, if you learn to channel it in the proper way, you could actually improve performance when it counts most. The record books are filled with the exploits of athletes who somehow reached beyond themselves in times of stressful competition. No wonder the business of professional sports deals with "performance anxiety management" and not just teaching technique.

But before you can really root out buck fever, a pair of deep-seated problems must be confronted. The first is a strong desire for success. Though I'm not suggesting that hunters exchange enthusiasm for indifference, I'm convinced that our thoughts must be focused on making the best possible shot, not "getting the animal." Put another way, concentrate on form rather than results. The more hung up you are about scoring, the more buck fever is apt to pay you an untimely visit.

Unfamiliarity is another root problem. As a general rule, experienced hunters are less likely to turn into Jell-O than beginners, as drawing upon past experiences in a familiar setting helps subdue stress. Again, in the sporting world, tested veterans typically outperform rookies when the game is on the line.

Dr. Greg Bambenek, a psychiatrist and avid deer hunter, recently made a startling discovery along these lines. In a laboratory experiment, he injected rats—trained to ring a bell five times to get some food—with increasing doses of adrenaline. Their ability to ring the bell decreased proportionately. "That was predictable," he said. "The strange part is that it took a much lower dose of adrenaline to discombobulate a rat, if it was in a novel, or unfamiliar, environment."

The Cure!

Curing, or at least controlling, buck fever starts with a changed outlook: Do not become obsessed with past failures or become preoccupied with tagging a buck or bull. Enjoy the hunt! Research shows that when obsession takes over, it can disrupt the body's natural healthy processes. An example of how the mind can block the body involves Harvard Medical School's Mind/Body Program for Infertility. After applying several mind-body approaches, one-third of the women became pregnant within six months of completing a course that did not emphasize getting pregnant.(It should be noted that participants of the program had previously tried, on the average, 3 1/2 years to become pregnant.)

Second, become as familiar as possible with real-life hunting situations. Remember Dr. Bambenek's rats. "It may sound corny, but repeated exposure to wild game is a good start, even [if it's] at a zoo or local pet farm," says John Weiss. "As my teenage son came of age, I made sure he saw plenty of tame deer before he hunted wild deer. It made a big difference observing deer, watching how they move, how they react."

Bob Foulkrod says that too many guys miss shots simply because they're afraid of missing. Ironically, the best antidote for fear of failure is success. And success starts at the practice range. The kind of practice that makes perfect involves shots you're likely to encounter in the woods. For example, if it's shooting out of a particular treestand hung at a certain height, rehearse it as often as it takes to make it second nature. For the mind and body to work in harmony, familiar messages

I'll never go moose hunting again without consulting the Man in the Moon—and I'll never again arrow a bull near water.

must be sent to the body and interpreted and carried out in milliseconds. The best way to achieve hand/eye coordination at the subconscious level is with constant repetition.

When the buck stops here, the link between the psyche and soma is most critical. You need a sound mind—in spite of adrenaline pumping in your veins. Over the years, hunters have tried a number of ploys to help them relax at the moment of truth. Most just complicate matters; some even backfire. The more you psych yourself into settling down, it seems, the more you focus on your nervous predicament, and the more panicky you become.

Take one old-timer's edict of "avoiding eye contact" with a big buck. Looking the other way is supposed to soothe raw nerves while preventing a deer's sixth sense from detecting your piercing gaze. It doesn't work. First of all, deer can't tell when they're being observed, as long as the hunter is hidden and downwind; a cat stalking a bird or mouse is nature's lesson that *focusing* is essential for hunting success. Worse yet, this antiquated advice merely stresses an already stressful situation. Bowhunters will inevitably rush the shot if they don't pick a spot on the animal's chest cavity and stay with it.

We can obtain better advice from psychosomatic medicine, which deals with the fascinating mind/body relationship. In recent years many major medical schools—Harvard, Stanford, Yale, UCLA—have established teaching departments devoted to mind/body medicine. Behavioral techniques, most notably "relaxation therapy" and "positive thought restructuring," can help hunters cope with stress.

Take hunters like my friend Tom, who succumb to hyperventilation. "[This] causes the blood to become alkaline," according to Dr. Gabe Merkin, with the Sportsmedicine Institute in Silver Springs, Maryland. "It opens the door to the symptoms of a panic attack."

To avoid this scenario, "square breathing" is common in hospital delivery rooms and on the basketball court, because it has therapeutic effects on the body and mind. "Take deep, measured breaths," says Dr. Manual Zane, professor of psychiatry and founder and director of the Phobia Clinic at the White Plains Hospital in New York. "This frees the brain and creates order out of chaos." Inhale and exhale at the same rate: Count to three or four, hold at this count, exhale at the same count. Repeat. Picture a square with equal sides representing each step of the breathing cycle. Another useful tactic you can count on is some timely subtraction. "Count backward from 1,000," says Dr. Zane. This gives the mind something to do without overloading it.

Next, deal the fear of failure a lethal blow by restructuring old, negative thoughts into positive images. See yourself doing exactly what you want to do (you've done so during practice, why not now?). Watch your arrow find its mark. Visualize flawless execution.

Now you can confidently pick a spot on an animal and blot everything else out. Experienced hunters block out the mesmerizing image of a huge rack, focusing instead on the animal's kill zone. Indeed, big-game hunters can be just as guilty of "flock shooting" as bird hunters if they forget to aim through the shot.

Buck fever is something we all must confront. Learn how to channel the extra energy in the proper direction, however, and you could become a *better* hunter. O

Help On The Pharm?

Dr. Greg Bambenek discovered that some individual rats handled increasing amounts of adrenalin better than others, suggesting that not all organisms—including humans—cope with stressful situations equally well. Preventive measures might help. For one, avoid known stimulants such as caffeine and nicotine. Another possible solution, Dr. Bambenek says, might be prescription drugs such as Inderal" (propranolol), to keep the heart rate and blood pressure in check.

"I've treated several patients [with this drug], achieving the same kind of results that dramamine gives sufferers of motion sickness," he said. "But before you head for the hunting woods, make sure you won't experience any side-effects." Drowsiness is one such possibility.

Because the symptoms of buck fever vary from person to person, what works for some might not work for others. Consider the following:

- Hyperventilation, or overbreathing, can lead to dizziness because of carbon dioxide "blow off." An old trick is breathing into a paper bag to quickly replenish lost carbon dioxide. This may not be practical in a hunting situation, however, so curl your arm around your face and breathe into the sleeve of your coat or jacket.

- Exercise can burn off excess adrenaline, which, in turn, generally subdues its unnerving symptoms. If this is impractical, try tightening and relaxing large muscles, particularly the thighs and back.

- Fears may originate in the ears, not mind, says Dr. Harold Levinson, psychiatrist, neurologist and co-author of the book, "Phobia Free". After researching 20,000 patients over 20 years, Dr. Levinson believes that 90 percent of all phobic behavior can be linked to an inner-ear malfunction. If in doubt, schedule an appointment with an ear specialist.

Chapter 13

MY SECRET SCENT

So far I haven't said much about the use of scents, other than explaining how offensive odors are produced and what are the best methods of controlling them. But in recent years I've been perfecting a scent system that's evolved into one of the most intriguing discoveries of my hunting career. In fact, it's right up there with knowing how to take advantage of the moon. I've been reluctant to go public with this phenomenon largely because it's controversial, and I didn't want it to detract from my main message on moon hunting. Indeed, what I'm about to share probably conflicts with much of what you've heard and read about using scents to attract deer. But now that tens of thousands of hunters are using the Moon Guide and Rut Guide to time their hunts efficiently, the time is ripe for a new chapter on deer attractants.

But first, a disclaimer: Just because I say it's so doesn't make it true. I want you to put the concepts in this chapter to work in your hunting area. Don't take my word for it; prove it to yourself. My philosophy on hunting is that if I'm right about something, other hunters should be able to reproduce results in the real world of big-game hunting in their own backyards.

Kicking Butt in Kansas

The defining moment in the refinement process of this scent system occurred several years ago while I was bowhunting and filming in Kansas during a November last Quarter Moon (one of my favorite lunar periods). I'd staked a Deer Rear decoy, which is essentially the back half of a foam deer body, to a low bush about 25 yards from my treestand. Then I set its Tail-Wagger, an ingenious battery-operated "tail flicker," to trip at eight-second intervals. Before scaling my treestand, I placed my secret potion 20 yards upwind and 20 yards downwind. I took the extra time to think through this setup because I couldn't cover both sides of a nearby hedge row; I wanted to give the 12-pointer I'd been playing cat 'n' mouse with something to think about, should he take the wrong fork in the trail.

Although the buck failed to show, a doe accompanied by a button buck came by around twilight. The doe walked up to the decoy, then button-hooked directly downwind of me. Of course she stomped, whistled, and snorted when the decoy failed to stomp, whistle, and snort back. Eventually she led her fawn past me . . . only to double-back again.

This all took place while both deer were mostly downwind of me and my videographer, Craig Hall, who captured the episode on tape. On the way back to the pickup, Hall exclaimed, "I've never seen a deer so completely fooled in my life!" From that point on, he vowed, he'd give decoying a serious try and would never again hunt without my pet potion.

So what's my secret lure? Although it consists of 100 percent authentic deer parts, you can't buy it in any sporting-goods store nor can you order it from a mail-order catalog. But if you hunt whitetails in areas where you can get doe tags, you're staring at a bountiful supply. All you have to do is bag a doe and apply some whitetail biology discovered recently by researchers at the University of Georgia.

If you REALLY want to fool deer, use a buck decoy and my secret scent; a McKenzie 3-D target doubles up as an effective deer deke.

Tarsal Glands Are Special

Deer possess four external glands that are part of a communication system that enables them to distinguish individual animals within a herd. In terms of practical hunting implications, the least significant is the metatarsal gland (located just above the dew claws), followed by the interdigital gland (located between the hooves), followed the preorbital gland (tear duct glands). Despite this, many commercial deer lures include some of these ingredients. Hock glands are different. Known technically as tarsal glands for their location at the tarsal joint (elbow) of the hind legs, these glands can help hunters lure deer within range from considerable distances. And they are effective before, during, and after the rut. Can you say this about the scent you're currently using?

Before we proceed, we need to make an important distinction: We're not

much interested in the tarsal glands of male deer. Instead, the tarsal glands of female deer form the foundation of the strategy I'm about to disclose. Most hunters seem to know that the most effective formulation for attracting bucks generally includes key agents produced by female, not male deer. Yet just about every hunter I've talked to who has experimented with tarsal glands has majored on buck tarsals. Why, why, why? Buck-derivative lures are not necessarily a waste of time -- you need them to doctor scrapes and spruce up rub lines -- but during the bulk of the hunting season bucks are preoccupied with monitoring the estrus cycle of does, not the testosterone levels of other bucks.

This buck is rub-urinating. So do does in order to re-charge their tarsal glands.

The tarsal glands extracted from does will not spook other does. Don't underestimate this! I can't count the times I've had a thick-racked buck follow a doe heading straight for my stand when, without warning, my grand plan turned to dust; typically, the doe catches a whiff of something she doesn't like (such as a commercial "estrus scent" placed near the trail) and veers off, taking the buck with her. Which is to say that any scent attracting some deer while spooking others is a two-steps-forward, three-steps-backward proposition. Since day one I've been searching for a truly universal scent, and this is it.

If that's not enough, doe tarsal glands are notably pungent and remarkably durable. The best scent in the world is useless if a buck has a difficult time picking it up, which is the main problem with most formulations. Simply stated, they're not very potent. And even if they start out fresh and strong, they seem

169

Tarsal glands extracted from does are the best- and maybe the only-year-round, either-sex deer attractant.

to lose their vitality in the rain (dilution) or in direct sunlight (oxidation). Not so with tarsal glands. Like I said, they're special.

The Science of Tarsal Glands

A detailed explanation of precisely how tarsal glands function remains somewhat of a mystery to researchers, but they have discovered the process that gives them their unusually sharp odor. Coincidentally, even the human nose can distinguish individual deer by the scent of their tarsal glands. For example, if you want to know if a fresh bed was made by a buck or a doe, all you have to do is get on all fours and sniff the ground; a buck's bed smells putrid and rank, a doe's markedly less so. In the snow, the yellowish stains of a buck's tarsal glands continue to reek for days, and many are the times I've been fooled into thinking a buck was just around the corner only to stumble upon a day-old bed: Snow is a good preservative and therefore a very good dispenser of scent.

Truth be known, not all deer research results in practical insights for hunters. But studies conducted at the University of Georgia on the patterns of urination and rub-urination of female deer appear to have unearthed a heaping plateful of timely advice.

Topping the list is the fact that tarsal glands do not undergo chemical changes during the reproductive cycle. This means that tarsal glands removed from an estrus doe are no more seductive than those removed from a mid-cycle doe. I've long suspected this, and I proved it to myself a couple of Octobers ago when an impressive 10-pointer grunted his way to a tarsal gland hung on a tree branch below my stand. This particular gland was collected from a Wisconsin doe nearly a month earlier, so I knew the donor wasn't in heat. Yet the buck's body language said otherwise: grunt, grunt, grunt. So in spite of what you may have been told on the subject of pheromones and estrus scents, do not underestimate the value of fresh tarsal glands. They do not have to be collected during the rut to be effective on rutting bucks. In addition, tarsal glands collected during the rut are unlikely to spook does after the rut. It's a win-win scent system.

There's nothing mysterious about tarsal tufts, except the fact that they're the best scent vent known to man - cis-4-hydroxydodec-6-enoic acid lactone is selectively retained by the tufts.

The Georgia researchers also discovered that urine is the primary source of "tarsal scent," resulting from the whitetails' idiosyncratic habit of rub-urinating. Indeed, most hunters do not know that does rub-urinate just as bucks do: The does in the study group urinated about nine times per day and rub-urinated at least once and sometimes twice per day, on average. No big deal? Only if you stop here and don't dig a little deeper.

Turns out that when a doe rub-urinates onto her tarsal glands, a component within her urine (cis-4-hydroxydodec-6-enoic acid lactone) is "selectively retained" by the tarsal tufts onto a sticky substance, sebum. This is the mechanism in which tarsal glands send "signals" to other deer, telling them key biological information. Of course these signals change, depending on the season and the saturation of urinary components deposited onto the tarsal tufts which, in turn, is based on the amount of rub-urinating a particular animal engages in.

The practical implications for hunters are staggering. First and foremost is the fact that fat-soluble compounds, extracted from urine onto the tufts, are what deer apparently find attractive; by itself urine is, at best, an incomplete sentence. In other words, urine is merely the telegram, not the message. So if your deer pee strategies seem to confuse, not arouse, whitetails, it's because you are sending a garbled signal.

A case in point is how a buck usually can't tell if a doe is in heat unless he noses her rump. He can tell if she's getting close, but without coming in contact with critical olfactory stimuli he can't tell a fertile female (one willing to accept his advances) from a mid-cycle female (one that's sure to bolt). Older bucks with numerous breeding experiences know all about this and don't waste time chasing unreceptive does. Inexperienced adolescent bucks are different. This explains why some urine-based products occasionally attract younger, curious males while rarely eliciting responses from older, mature bucks who know exactly what they're looking for.

Equally important is how the tarsal gland's generous supply of sticky sebum makes for an ideal scent depository. Nothing compares to the way these glands "wick" the odor of deer urine; cotton and various synthetic "scent vents" can't come close to this natural scent dispersal system.

Deer Urine and Tarsal Glands

To be effective, tarsal glands require proper handling. The sebaceous glands within the tarsal tufts eventually decompose and lose their ability to strain key compounds from deer urine - which brings us to an interesting subject. Just as we've seen that straight deer urine isn't the most effective attractant, fresh deer urine can enhance the effectiveness of tarsal glands and even help extend their life. But when I say "fresh," I mean FRESH. I've tried "aged" deer urines, and they just don't measure up.

Keep in mind that urines quickly decompose and produce ammonia-type by-products that may overwhelm original compounds contained in fresh urine. Although ammonia is a natural by-product and evaporates rather quickly, it is not a whitetail stimulant.

What about anointing doe tarsal glands with so-called "estrus urine"? Considering the research cited along with empirical and anecdotal evidence, it doesn't seem to make much of a difference. Apparently the volatility of

This Iowa buck double-backed after getting a whiff of a pair of tarsal glands placed upwind and downwind of my treestand.

pheromones associated with the vaginal discharge of cycling does is sky-high, making the process of capturing and bottling these elusive compounds next to impossible.

Back to our little scheme. When mature bucks use their noses to locate receptive females, urine deposits scattered throughout the deer woods play a secondary role. Bucks do occasionally investigate groundscrapes, but most of the rutting bucks I've encountered in the wild held their noses high while sniffing out air currents. The lone exception is a buck hot on the track of a specific doe he's already zeroed in on. There's a particularly engaging segment in Moonbeams III that bears this out. While I was scouting a Wisconsin oak stand, I heard hooves pounding over the rise and immediately engaged the recorder button of my camcorder. Seconds later, a bruiser of a buck nearly bowled me over, totally oblivious to my presence. I filmed him doubling back in apparent confusion and looped around right in front of me. He was so close I could hear him sniffing like a hound on a coon's trail. This is why I've long abandoned the use of deer urine as a mainline scent strategy. But I can't say enough about fresh deer urine used in conjunction with tarsal glands. The difference is night and day, success and failure.

So the question begs, what's a good source of fresh deer urine? To begin, I'd

173

steer clear of commercial products stored in plastic containers. Their concave sides indicate the breakdown of ingredients and resultant gas leakage -- plastic is gas permeable--of ammonia. Glass-bottled urines last longer, and I believe refrigeration is a time-consuming but necessary step. Several companies now market fresh deer urine and date the packaging for consumer inspection. Another option is the bladder of a freshly harvested doe. Still another option is to go to a deer farm. In most instances they're licensed by their respective states, meaning their whereabouts is public information. Call the owner and I'll bet you can buy as much fresh doe pee as you can afford. This includes deer farmers who private label their deer urine to big-name companies.

Another clue to a urine's condition is its color. Back when I used to hunt the firearms season in northern Minnesota, I really dug into this subject. To make a technical story not so technical, I learned that one of the best ways to kill a buck was to track does in the snow. Not any old doe would do, either. Those with cranberry-stained urine discharges invariably led me to more bucks than those whose urine deposits were yellowish. Color can make a difference, although there are no hard and fast rules. Simple common sense suggests that yellow urine should be more fresh than brown or black urine, assuming the lure-maker isn't "doctoring" the ingredients with, say, deer droppings (don't laugh; this is a fairly common tactic that some swear by).

Tarsal Trickery

After hunting with tarsal glands for several seasons, I settled on a specific method for laying them out. Specifically, you'll get much better results by positioning them ABOVE ground -- waist- to chest-high is ideal -- rather than using the customary ground deposit commonly associated with commercial deer urines. An elevated position enhances air circulation and wafts scent more efficiently throughout the immediate area. Regarding specific locations, don't make it unnecessarily complicated: Simply place at least one tuft upwind and one tuft downwind from your stand or blind. Then get ready to be amazed: Believe it or not, I've observed many deer ignore my human scent as they focused on the tarsal glands around me. It's uncanny how deer react when encountering the scent of these glands.

Tarsal glands are easy to work with: Simply punch a hole through the hide and slip the tuft onto a twig. Or, wedge the tuft into the crotch of a tree branch or bush or sapling. Whatever you do, don't forget to remove the gland at the end of a day's hunt. Otherwise you could condition deer to the gland's scent and location while you're gone. This may take some forethought, such as knowing exactly where you left the things. One evening, for instance, I spent an exasperating hour trying to retrieve a "missing" tarsal gland with my flashlight. Never again: Nowadays I use Hunter's Specialties' Limb Lights (phosphorescent "twist strips") to pin the glands and simplify after-dark retrieval.

If you follow these guidelines, I guarantee that this scent system will turn heads -- not to mention racks. All it will take is a single encounter with a whitetail to see how a deer attractant is supposed to work. When you see it with your own eyes, here's betting you'll be hooked.

Getting TarSaled

Most hunters should have little difficulty collecting an adequate hunting supply of tarsal glands. Engage in doe management and get the word out in your hunting network. If your particular state records deer kills at registration sites, ask check-station officials to give you a call when deer are registered. In many states deer are registered almost daily throughout the fall.

But if time and distance are limiting factors, check out RealDeer from Shannon Outdoors. This commercial product is made from fresh body parts of, well, real deer. Product innovator Keith Shannon isn't exactly long-winded on just what's inside the pouches that attach conveniently to bushes and tree limbs. But I've taken enough of them apart to know that they include tarsal tufts and hair from key areas of a deer's hide. Firsthand experience proved to me that RealDeer is the real deal; however, as I write this, RealDeer might be phased out and replaced by a liquid form that reportedly doesn't compromise its vitality and won't break down inside a bottle. For more information, contact Shannon Outdoors, PO Box 444, Louisville, GA 30434; 800/852-8058.

Finally, freshly extracted tarsal glands must be handled with extreme care. Always refrigerate them overnight during hunts and freeze them between hunts. If you store them in a tightly sealed heavy-duty plastic bag (squeeze out all of the air) you can retard oxidation and prevent freezer burn. The tufts should last several months.

Testing Tarsals: Don't Trust Your Nose

One of the most fascinating characteristics of tarsal glands is the way they smell. Or don't smell. Or smell perfumy. Or stink like a barnyard. No two glands smell alike. Even my nose can differentiate two specimens. The implication for hunters is that deer, like humans, are individuals; each has its unique olfactory signature. So just because a particular tarsal gland doesn't reek with deer-like odors, don't assume it won't attract bucks.

Just as your nose can't tell a "hot" tarsal gland from an also-ran, it can't be trusted when sniffing out older, used tarsal glands. I've achieved startling results with tarsal tufts that were three months old, even though they smelled a lot stronger when I first collected them. You just have to put them to the test and let the deer tell you which ones trip their trigger.

Buck Tarsals

The best all-purpose scent for hunting bucks is the tarsal gland from a female deer; however, buck tarsal glands have their place if you follow a few precautions.

The best setup naturally involves a scrape – make that a FRESH scrape. With a tarsal gland hanging near the licking branch, you can create the illusion of an invader taking over a resident's scraping territory. Research indicates that bucks visit scrapes adorned with licking branches more often than scrapes without them, so make a licking branch – bend a branch or bring your own – if the scrape is branch-less.

I also recommend dragging the tuft (attached to a string) through the scrape. Additionally, you can transform the tuft into a drag rag or even string a pair of tufts together – one from a doe, one from a buck – and troll them in the immediate area..

Chapter 14

THE NAME'S MURRAY, NOT MURPHY

Whether you realize it or not, humans are governed by a set of universal laws that don't depend on mere mortals for enforcement. I'm not talking about the principles of gravity or relativity, or theorems like "if A equals B and B equals C, A equals C." I can cope with those laws. Instead, I'm referring to the infamous 1949 discovery by George E. Nichols. It seems aircraft engineer Ed Murphy observed that a fellow technician always seemed to find a way to "do it wrong." Nichols refined this keen observation into Murphy's Law.

No doubt you've been fleeced by Murphy's most-oft-quoted law, "If something can go wrong, it will." Or you might be more familiar with equally binding laws, such as "Nothing is as easy as it looks" and "Everything takes longer than you think it will." What does this have to do with deer hunting? A lot.

Murphy seems to have reserved a plethora of laws for humble, hard-working hunters who deserve better. I've concluded that my name has somehow become a serious handicap—Murray sounds too much like Murphy—and that I'm one of Murphy's favorite targets. Rational explanations pale against the kind of treatment I've suffered of late.

Another possibility is that I'm on the brink of a breakthrough discovery—there could be Murray's Laws floating around out there. My wife says these things happen to everybody and that I'm just feeling sorry for myself. I don't think so. I'm not the self-pity type. Besides, the stories I bring home from deer camp more than raise eyebrows at the bow shop. Indeed, my credibility is at stake: They are just highfalutin excuses for not filling my deer tag, the guys say.

Now, that hurts. As the Lord is my witness, I don't have to embellish the stories. Below are a few samples for you to mull over. Check them out, and let me know if these things happen to you, too. First, let me warn you that some of the incidents are going to sound a bit outlandish. But they're all true. I'm not under the influence of one of Murphy's less-than-discreet laws, "Nothing is so insignificant that it can't be blown out of proportion."

Briefly, there are three branches of Murphy's Laws concerning hunting. One serves to make life miserable as you get there (wherever "there" may be), the next deals with the hunt itself, and the third plagues you on your way home.

Getting There Laws (That Really Get You)

Some of my worst dealings with Murphy have occurred before I stepped out the door. Like the time I wanted a pair of silk underwear for a September bowhunt. Most astute hunters know that silk makes a dandy early season, next-to-the-skin garment. Its insulation index is perfect for moderate temperatures, and its smooth texture stretches nicely without constricting body movement—an ideal combination for bowhunting when evenings are cool and afternoons are warm.

Well, I had my heart set on silk undies, specifically a Large top and a Medium bottom. What a mistake. As Murphy would have it, every mail-order house I called was back-ordered in my sizes. I could purchase a Medium top and a Large bottom or two Larges or two Mediums—any combination except the one I wanted.

Coincidence? On the surface, perhaps. Dig a little deeper, however, and the potential for a sinister plot emerges. Exhibit A: My brother, who doesn't bowhunt but "just wanted to try the stuff," called the evening before I was to leave for my trip to tell me he got his order filled without any hassle. Exhibit B: A hunting buddy also phoned me that night, explaining that a local mail-order company had just received a big shipment of silk underwear in all sizes. Of course, I had to hit the road by 5 the next morning before the store opened.

Call this the MAIL-ORDER LAW: *The size (or color or model) you want will always be back-ordered or discontinued.*

OK, OK. No big deal. A guy ought to be able to live without silk underwear. At least it won't cost a buck (we'll get to that, but I just wanted to set the stage).

Now I'm out the door and heading down the highway. I'm packed to the hilt and singing along with Amy Grant and some Yes oldie-but-goodies. Nebraska is a 16-hour away drive from my home in northern Minnesota. A long haul, but I like the drive. Some of the backroads snaking through Badlands country are as scenic—and desolate—as they get. Everything went unusually smoothly until the segment of the trip when I discovered one of Murphy's travel laws.

As I coasted down a steep grade, a highway sign warned of a narrow bridge at the bottom of the hill. On the distant horizon, I could make out another rather imposing hill, so I punched the gas peddle to make the grade with my slightly underpowered rig.

Enter an 18-wheel, horn-tootin' semi in 12th gear steam-rolling my way. Of course, the bridge was too narrow for a pair of Ferrari Testarossas, let alone me and the trucker. Someone had to give, and it wasn't going to be the trucker. Frantically, I stomped on the brakes with both feet, skidding my pickup right and left out of control. Either I had come to a halt in front of the bridge, or I would careen over the embankment into the White River. I barely made it.

For the record, that truck was the only vehicle I saw on that leg of the trip, so THE NARROW BRIDGE LAW strikes again: A *car and a semi, traveling in opposite directions on a desolate road, will always meet at the narrowest bridge in the region.*

I was about four hours from deer camp now. I was starving. That hair-raising episode at the bridge took a lot out of me. Time for a relaxing bite to eat. Luckily (I'm being sarcastic) the church in the next town was sponsoring an all-you-can-eat buffet; the basement was filled with the aroma of smoked ham, roast turkey, home-baked pie and fresh-brewed coffee. My stomach was growling like a

Rottweiler as the long line inched slowly forward.

I spied my favorite dessert, fresh pecan pie, right away. Only one problem: There were about three dozen people in line ahead of me and only three pieces of pecan pie left.

Well, precisely the 35th person—the guy immediately in front of me—scooped up the last piece of pecan pie. Interestingly, he mumbled something about changing his mind at the last instant, rejecting a much larger slice of cherry pie (which I'm allergic to).

There To Get You Laws (When You Get There)

Travel laws only make life difficult; laws affecting the hunt make life miserable. Some of these laws deal with does, and some deal with bucks. Some govern equipment, and some have jurisdiction over environmental factors, including, but not limited to, tree branches, shooting light and weather. These are universal, affecting all deer hunters, I admit, but they seem to hound me out of proportion. It's as if the laws of probability are suspended when I'm in the woods.

Take the time I'd been in my treestand, silent as a ghost for several hours, monitoring a line of scrapes leading out of a cedar swamp. From nowhere, an uncontrollable urge to cough gripped me. I wasn't nursing a sore throat or cold; I couldn't have felt better. Still, the tickling feather in my throat became increasingly unbearable and, after fighting it back for 20, maybe 30 seconds, I had to cough. So I buried my head in my right forearm and let it rip.

In the sterile silence of the woods, I held my breath, praying that a nearby buck wouldn't hear my rude, intruding cough. But that which I feared came upon me: A buck bolted behind me, whistling shrill warnings as he disappeared in the cedar boughs. What timing. THE TIME TO COUGH IT UP LAW is nothing to sneeze at.

An interesting corollary to this covers those seemingly insignificant complications that crop up at the last possible instant. Like the time I bowhunted prairie whitetails in South Dakota. On the first night of the hunt, Bob Stalley and I had glassed some dandy whitetails in the distance. We let the animals settle down and hung a portable treestand at a bottleneck in a brushy creek bottom. I'll never forget what unfolded when I returned that evening.

The sky was pink as a baby's bottom when the doe and her fawn dawdled down the beaten deer trail in front of me. She stopped broadside, 15 paces away, licked the air and swished her tail. The fawn shadowed close behind, and neither had a clue of my presence. What a golden moment. With nocked arrow and helium expectations, I savored every second.

When the buck appeared silhouetted against a deepening rose sky, well, what could be rosier? Like a fairy tale, the 140-class 10-pointer followed the footsteps of the doe and fawn which had given no warning that this wasn't a safe place to be. As he tested the evening thermals, I confidently whispered under my breath, *Go ahead, you're upwind.* That's when the buck suddenly hit the brakes. His ears twirled like radar dishes, his neck craned over his shoulder. He turned inside out and vanished over the hill.

Moseying my way was the only thing that could possibly louse up my magic moment. *Moo-oo. Moo-oo-ah.* Why that cow chose this instant to feed in "my" creek bottom is beyond me. But Murphy knew.

There's more. My entire hunt was "udderly" ruined. That cow, along with another 200 head, played follow-the-leader with Stalley and me the next four days. And as any savvy prairie deer hunter knows, you can't push whitetails out of the brush and bowhunt them effectively. So watch out for the COW COROLLARY: *Nothing is so bad that it can't get worse.*

Besides cows, does can get in your way and ruin an otherwise perfectly orchestrated game plan. Like the time I'd located a staging area where bucks milled around before hitting a lush alfalfa field after dark. It was a brilliant setup, considering the field edge would be a doe-and-fawn pony show, and locating too close to daytime bedding areas would spook deer in the noisy underbrush.

The woods floor of the staging area was carpeted with enough Boston-bean-sized droppings to fertilize a potato farm. Nearby rubs on eight to 10-inch balsams screamed "Hunt here, *now!*" Because there were no trees large enough to support a portable stand, I pitched a Hide 'um Hunter five-pole blind downwind from a hot trail intersection.

About a half-hour before sunset, a doe bounced merrily down the trail. She paused briefly at the intersection before continuing on in front of me. As she passed within 12 paces of my blind, she began nibbling on aspen shoots and gradually fed out of sight. She was barely visible when another doe mimicked her—prancing down the lane, pausing at the intersection, proceed along the trail in front of me.

This looked too good to be true. I had bamboozled a pair of matriarchs, and any buck coming down the pike would surely follow suit.

Sure enough, moments later a forkhorn followed the script to a T—pausing at the intersection, taking the lower fork, feeding nonchalantly in front of my blind. Just as he disappeared, another buck popped into view. The handsome nine-pointer lowered his head and half-trotted down the trail like all of the deer preceding him. Of course, he didn't make it to the intersection.

Out of nowhere, a doe took cuts in front of him. Her cocked tail and agitated body language said she was "itchy." For no apparent reason, she decided to take the upper fork. Needless to say, the buck followed in hot pursuit. As is often the case when dealing with Murphy, there's insult to be added to injury—an equally impressive buck materialized just as the nine-pointer disappeared. This fellow looked like a dog on a chain when he caught a whiff of the frisky doe. Up the trail he bounced. Murphy won again.

Female deer, like females in general, are a strange lot, especially during the rut. Watch out for the PERVERSELY PERVASIVE DOE LAW: *If it looks too good to be true, it is.*

Bucks are equally susceptible to Murphy's Laws. Consider the LAW OF WHITETAIL SYMMETRY. One fine November evening, I discovered how this law affects serious buck hunting when I joined Iowa guide John Hambleton. (Hambleton and I also discovered a myriad of other laws, which shall be held in strict confidence until the hunting community is ready for them.)

The very first night of the hunt, a wide-beamed buck zigzagged under my treestand. Oblivious to my presence, he riveted his attention to a pair of does feeding upwind in a picked cornfield. At about 15 yards, he stopped broadside.

As I silently drew my bow, however, I couldn't help but notice that his rack was deformed—the left side sported five tall, bone-white tines, but the right side looked like a comb with missing teeth. Hence, the SYMMETRY LAW: *Half a rack does not a trophy make.*

The HOT STAND RULE proved deadly in Minnesota in December. Mike Kohler invited me to join him for a "metro bowhunt" in the suburbs of Minneapolis, where one particular stand had produced a pair of Pope and Young bucks the previous month. "For every doe you'll see," he whispered in the pre-dawn darkness, "you'll see at least eight bucks. The buck-to-doe ratio is unreal."

Well, I saw four does and no bucks (I can't wait to see the racks on the next 32 bucks the next time I hunt with Kohler). A bit discouraged, I left for home that evening, but Kohler continued to bowhunt. A day later, he called. "Would you believe a 140-class eight-pointer?" he chirped. "You should have hunted one more day, Murray." Of course. THE HOT STAND RULE scores again: A *stand is always hot when you're not in it.*

Incidentally, a close corollary is the RIGHT STAND, WRONG TIME LAW that I rediscovered one January morning while bowhunting Willow Point Lodge, on the Mississippi/Louisiana border. I miscommunicated with guide Billy Jones the last morning of the hunt (when my good ol' boy buddies chew snuff, my Minnesota ears don't handle the dialect well). Anyhow, I ended up at the wrong stand. Needless to say, the one Jones tried to steer me to was the "right" one— the "biggest buck the crew had seen in weeks" was glassed underneath it that morning.

The laws that govern mechanical equipment are the most frustrating of all. You should be able to control these variables but, as the following illustrates, you can't.

One sublime October afternoon, I enjoyed the view from my 25-foot-high portable. As I glanced below, however, something caught the corner of my eye. My bowstring serving was beginning to unravel—a common plight when monofilament serving slips as Fast Flight string material creeps. Vivid images of a blown serving at the moment of truth flashed across my mind, so I removed my mechanical release and tore into the project with both hands. My watch read 1:30 p.m. The little five-minute task of tightening the gaps within the serving shouldn't hurt, I figured; the Moon time for that day wasn't until 2:20. Well, the bottom pigtail pulled free, and it took me about an hour to jury rig a knot precariously held together by an Eliminator Button.

The project cost me. A buck trotted out to my right as I cinched up the knot. All I could do was freeze and hope he'd return, which he didn't. Next time you think you've got time to burn on a treestand, remember THE BALLOON LAW: *Work expands to fill unavailable space.*

Which reminds me of the time I dropped my mechanical release while munching on a granola bar. Fingers shooters laugh at stories like this, but I've usually got a good rebuttal: a backup release conveniently stowed in my backpack. Or so I thought, this time around. The deeper I dug into my four-compartment Tracker Pack, the more exasperated I got. If a buck moved within range at this precise moment, I could handle it, because I practice with bare fingers and know that my shot hits slightly high and right with a shoot-through arrow rest. But I couldn't handle what happened next.

After carefully panning the landscape, I quietly unbuckled my safety belt and climbed down to retrieve my release. As I stooped down to pick it up, my eyes met those of a curious buck. He had me. I call this law NEWTON'S BOMB: *For every action, there is an equal and opposite calamity.*

Binding Laws When Homeward Bound

Finally, the laws affecting travel back home. I'll leave you with one of many examples. Following a successful hunt out West, my flight was delayed due to poor visibility at take-off time. When I arrived in Minneapolis a tad late, Murphy seized the moment and saw to it that my connecting flight was unusually punctual; I missed it by five minutes. Hence, the AIRLINE CAHOOTS LAW: *Whenever your flight is late, your connecting flight will always be on, or ahead of, schedule.* (Naturally, the reverse is also true.)

So tell me, do these things happen to you, too, or am I just lucky?

Testimonials

I get letters. And phone calls. And faxes. And e-mail. Correspondence keeps piling up, telling me what I already know: Hunt by the Moon! Take a recent phone call from Donald Ludwig. He was skeptical, so he undertook a little experiment. "I live near a deer-check station in Salisbury, North Carolina," he said. "So I compared the registration dates and times with those of your [Moon] Guide. I was amazed: Of about 400 deer registered, nearly all were taken when the Guide listed favorable times for morning or evening hunting. So few deer were registered on days with midday Moon [times] that I just knew I had to start hunting by the Moon."

Here's a cross-section of hunter-feedback I've received:

- "Like lots of veteran deer hunters, I had my doubts. But during the '94 season I gradually became a believer. You can bet I'll be including the [Moon Guide] in all my pre-planning preparations."—M.R. James, founder and editor of *Bowhunter.*

- "I killed two bucks in the Piedmont area of the Blue Ridge Mountains using your Moon [Guide]."—Roger Moffler, Bedford, VA.

- "It seems as though the deer have read the [Moon] Guide and have adopted it as a dinner bell. We scheduled our hunting times around the Guide and succeeded in taking 11 deer between three of us. My buddies now call up asking, 'What time are the deer coming out tomorrow?'"—Steve Moquin, Athens, AL.

- "I totally believe in it."—Tom Storm, book author, video producer, Great Falls, MT.

- "Thanks for some good information. I had told several of the hunters at camp about the [Moon Guide] but I guess they didn't believe me until I brought in my deer."—Warren Holland, Monterey, LA.

- "The more you think about it, the more sense it makes."—Russell Thornberry, editor, *Buckmasters.*

- "My brother and I hunted a spot near his home that we always considered a morning-only spot. It's a transition zone, and your Moon Guide showed activity there for [an afternoon hunt] on November 7 and 8. This concurs with what actually happened... I hope this becomes a general rule!"—Charles LaVersa, Newburyport, MA.

- "Definitely the hottest whitetail news since rattling."—Jerry Johnston, Founder & Publisher, *Texas Trophy Hunters.*
- "[The Guide] will force you to break with tradition, but you'll be glad you did."—Mike Langin, Wisconsin trophy bowhunter.
- "After reading [your thoughts on the Moon] I decided to check [the Guide's] validity. I was astounded at the accuracy—not only were the times accurate, but the [predicted] placement was as well. I realize that no single factor determines whitetail movement, but having another piece of the puzzle helps."—Dan Mathews, Camden, SC.
- "With your Moon Guide, good weather and a good hunting area that has big bucks... you are bound to improve success on a big buck."—Steve Shoop, J & S Hunting Club, Memphis, MO.

Russ Thornberry with a nice midday buck.

- "This is the best season my partner and I have ever had, thanks to your [information]."—Danny Woods, Pinnacle, NC.
- "Thanks for publishing [the information on the Moon]. Enclosed is a photo of my 10-point, 270-pound whitetail. The deer was shot at 3:15 on November 6, 1994, and according to the Moon Guide prime time was 3:10. This is the second buck to fall to the Guide this season."—David Shumway, Batavia, IL.
- "To put it simply, we were absolutely amazed. We saw deer movement nearly every outing at the appointed time, plus or minus one hour. Hope you sell a lot of Guides, but not in Haywood County."—Mark Kendrick, Brownsville, TN.
- "Like fish [activity], deer movement is strongly linked to the Moon's position. I can't wait to use your Moon Guide in future hunting plans. You've predicted deer movements with astounding accuracy."—Bill Jordan, Spartan-Reatree.
- "I caught [a 180-class] buck sneaking by at 8:30 a.m. right when the Moon said he would, so I watched where he bedded and got him. Yeah, I'm a believer."—Rich McCauley, NE.
- "After a week-long Iowa bowhunt last fall, all but one of my party's nine hunters became believers. The only skeptic asked to borrow my Moon Guide when I left camp."—Mike Finé.
- "Over a two-day stretch every one of us had

Mike Langin with his huge Minnesota non-typical whitetail.

action. I mean, we either had shots or tagged a deer. When the Moon Guide said deer wouldn't show up [next to food sources] it wasn't kidding—we never saw deer when we weren't supposed to."—Glen Nelson, president of the Flathorn Hunting Club, based in Alabama's Monroe County.

• "[As a] hunting advisor for Browning and field-tester for many other companies, I'm not [easily] impressed with every gadget I get my hands on. But it looks like you're onto something! Last fall Hank Williams Jr. called me just about every night for a month to find out when the best time was to go hunting. I finally gave him a copy of your Moon Guide.—Brenda Valentine, Buchanan, TN.

More Good Info

GREAT SAUSAGE RECIPES AND MEAT CURING *by Rytek Kutas*. If you enjoy venison vittles as much as the Murray household, this book is a must. The Sausage Maker, 26 Military Road, Buffalo, NY 14207 (716-876-5521). A short-cut that's long on flavor is Spice 'n Slice's slick mix-shape-bake system; all of the ingredients come in one package. Grandma LaMure's Spice 'n Slice, P.O. Box 26051, Phoenix, AZ 85068-6051 (602-861-4094).

Honest, humble, hard-working guides are hard to find for western hunts. Tom Klumker is the exception to this rule. If he has an opening to bowhunt elk in New Mexico or Arizona, book it: San Francisco Outfitters, HC 61, Box 179-C, Glenwood, NM 88039; (505-539-2517; www.gilanet.com/sfroutfitters).

The best-run *trophy* whitetail bowhunting operation I've tasted in the US is Steve Shoop's camp headquartered in northern Missouri and southern Iowa. J & S Trophy Hunts, Box 312, Memphis, MO 63555 (660-945-3736).

Joe and Amy Gizdic are a rare, down-to-earth outfitters in the Midwest with a knack for putting customers onto big bucks; Tall Tine Outfitters (217-589-6990).

My good friend (and co-author of my book, How To Win The Walleye Game) Mike McClelland has gotten into outfitting. South Dakota, North Dakota are his big backyard. Cheyenne Ridge Outfitters & Lodge, 216 S. Frontier Rd., Ft. Pierre, SD 57532 (800-223-9126; www.cheyenneridge.com).

Most big-buck outfitters in Canada cater primarily to gun hunters and secondarily to bowhunters. Here's a pair that services both well. Arnold Holmes' Saskatchewan whitetail camp encompasses 300 square miles and boasts a 1:1 buck-to-doe ratio with super genetics. Dahl Creek Outfitters, Box 645, Hudson Bay, Saskatchewan, Canada S0E 0Y0 (306-865-2097). Expect a great hunt from Harvey McDonald, too. Elusive Saskatchewan Whitetail Outfitters, Rural Route #1, Richard, Saskatchewan, Canada S0M 2P0 (306-246-4788).

Dennis Hindbo's Tamarack Vista Outfitting in Alberta is a good example of good people doing a good job of providing good hunting: Dennis & Susan Hindbo, Junction 54 & 22 (E of Caroline), Box 411, Caroline, Alberta Canada T0M 0M0; 800-387-2836. ⚬